of the AGE OF ASPARAGUS

Give Peas a Chance!

CHEF WENDELL FOWLER

BRZAMO PUBLISHING, LLC

BRZAMO PUBLISHING, LLC
8338 Tequista Court
Indianapolis, Indiana 46236
www.brazamo.com

ISBN 0-9743580-9-6

Library of Congress Control Number 2004105475

Book design by Sheila Samson, WordCrafter, Inc., Carmel, Indiana
Front cover art by Dave Fowler, Fowler Photography, Inc., Ogallala, Nebraska
Back cover art by Daren Baker, Bothell, Washington, dbdesignsit@msn.com

---

Also by Chef Wendell Fowler:

Eat Right, Now! Recipes for a Healthy Lifestyle

(Emmis Books, ISBN 1-57860-104-5) *$16.95*

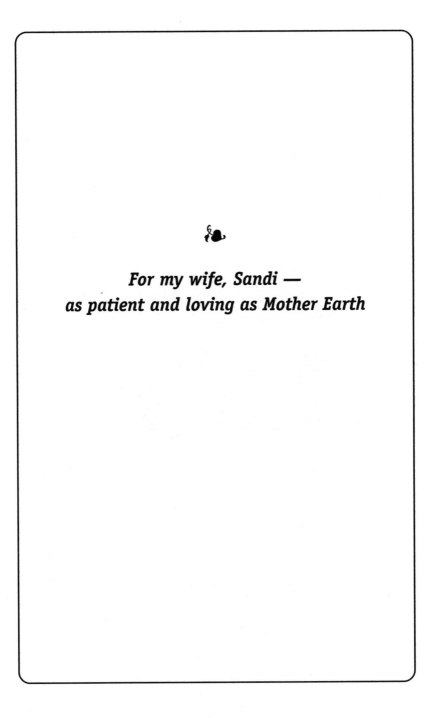

For my wife, Sandi —
as patient and loving as Mother Earth

Contents

FOREWORD vii

ACKNOWLEDGMENTS viii

ξ🐑

ECO-FOODS ESSAYS AND EDITORIALS

Live Long and Prosper 3

Food in the Name of Celebration:
    A Nutritional Paradox 6

Teaching An Old Dog New Tricks: *It's Never Too Late*
    To Go Vegetarian 11

Asparagus Tips 16

Breakfast: *Jumpstart Your Brain* 23

Take Two Apples and Call Me In the Morning:
    Getting to the Core of the Matter 28

Chocolate: *The Opiate of the Masses* 34

Diabetes: *A Pandemic of Modern Society* 42

Cheese: *Don't Let the Curds Get in the Whey* 47

Probiotics: *Our First Line of Defense in*
    the Warring Garden of Eatin' 53

Quinoa: *The Mother Grain* 58

"Live" Food: *The Taste of Life* 63

Honey: *The Other Vitamin Bee?* 68

"Liquid Candy": *The Cold Hard Truths About Soft Drinks* 73

Urban Tumbleweeds: *America's Love Affair with Littering* 78

Sex and Food: *Or, Eating for Pleasure* 83

Tea: *The Civilized Beverage* 87

Soy: *Is It the Perfect Food, or Does Tofu Have an Evil Twin?* 92

There's a Fungus Among Us! Shiitakes: *The Heart-smart Food of the Future* 97

Garlic: *Let's Make a Stink Out of This Issue* 101

Potent Pumpkin Power 107

THE RECIPES

TIPS FOR HEALTHY EATING 111

HEALTHY CONVERSIONS 112

APPETIZERS, SNACKS, AND BEVERAGES 115

SOUPS, SALADS, AND SAUCES 127

BEANS, GRAINS, AND PASTA 153

CASSEROLES AND ENTREES 171

SIDE DISHES 185

DESSERTS 201

INDEX 217

Foreword

Pick up any newspaper or magazine or flip on your local or national news and the reality will hit you in the face: We're getting fatter.

Our hectic lives, lack of exercise, and the "supersizing" of America is taking a toll on us—physically and spiritually.

I had the good fortune to meet Wendell Fowler about three years ago when I was searching for a new food columnist for *Indianapolis Prime Times*, a newspaper for people fifty and older. I knew Wendell had the credentials I was looking for—former newspaper reporter, accomplished chef—but what I didn't learn until later was Wendell's passion for healthy eating.

We've shared stories of growing up in the "Age of Aquarius," the crazy, let-it-all-hang-out days of the 1960s. Wendell is man who knows from experience what poor diet and lack of exercise can do, and he is the first to admit that his lifestyle in those days almost killed him. After receiving the news from his doctor that he was suffering from cardiomyopathy, Wendell took charge of his life, embracing a vegetarian diet and starting a daily exercise regime. The result? He shed one hundred pounds, and has become a healthy, energetic, walking testament to food as medicine.

With the zeal of an evangelist, Wendell guides us down the path of "right-stuff" eating. He's a man with a mission—to spread the message that it's never too late to make healthy, positive changes in your life.

Della Pacheco
Editor, *Indianapolis Prime Times*
and *Cincinnati Fifty plus!*

Acknowledgments

Mother dearest has yet to deny the assumption that I was weaned on a tongue sandwich, and through the passage of years, I've been informed, repeatedly, that I could talk the edamame off the vine.

Therefore, it is most fortuitous that I make my living preaching (evangelizing?), sharing, writing, cooking, and oratorically pontificating on the virtues of eating in harmony with nature. *My* muse for the evolution from a traditional escofier, or "cream-and-butter" chef to an eco-friendly chef, motivational speaker, syndicated "health" columnist, humorist, and author, was born in 1988, from an unexpected, albeit, inciting kiss, square on the lips, from the Grim Reaper. The symptoms: atrial fibrillation, a resting heart rate of 155, no regular heartbeat, and congestive heart failure underscored by eight pounds of fluid sloshing around my puny, overtaxed, gelatinous heart. The diagnosis: viral cardiomyopathy. *Mr. Fowler, you are going to die. Get prepared.*

My plans differed, however, and I proceeded to cut through the negativity, engage my psycho-physiological connection, kicked death's ugly, wrinkled butt, and launched a victorious, proactive assault on my dying heart.

The Great Creator had my rapt attention. In retrospect, knocking me upside the head with a harrowing close encounter with death was a blessing and a rare second chance in life to get it right! An experience like that can be rather motivating. *Wendell, you don't get it—I'm not finished with you yet!* Yes, God.

My eyes were opened PDQ. My life's purpose was revealed as the creaking, unlubricated doors of my mind opened to the grandeur and bounty of the earth. It was a time to accept my mission.

Losing a whopping one hundred pounds and major life trauma tends to weed out some so-called friends, which can be good for our souls to search themselves, evaluate, and tactfully clean house. For example, at various social engagements I would often hear whispers in the background: "Hey. What's wrong with Wendell?" queried one portly man busy juggling a bacon and liver rumaki in one hand and a double scotch in the other. "He's so thin. Looks ailing." "Must . . . cough . . . have AIDS or cancer," answered his chain-smoking buddy. "He can't be healthy. Got a light?"

"Daggonit it, I'm healthy! That's what's 'wrong' with me," I would mutter to myself. Considering that almost two-thirds of Americans are overweight, it's no wonder I stand out like a sore thumb.

After completing cardio rehab, as I gradually eased back into society, I soon discovered my true allies. I was pleasantly surprised by those left standing: my loyal, loving family; members of my village; and loyal business peers and colleagues.

Call me an idealistic, people-pleasing eccentric if you will. I love people, cherish spending social time with my family and community, kibitzing, learning about life, sharing knowledge, bragging, holding court, telling bad jokes, networking, and being genuinely interested in their needs, concerns, and contributions to our village. We can all agree that socializing in a friendly environment makes humans healthier. The wacky, unpredictable human animal is transformed by mingling and associating with other humans. The socializing role of community is important in the health, peace, and sanity of our turbulent modern world.

The phrase "sense of community" seems to be on everyone's lips. Do you recognize the valuable services of your community, and recognize and treasure their contributions that supports your family's physical well-being, mental health, the quality of their lifestyle, and ultimately, their peace of mind?

My own social and business community is one, large, extended family, and that is something quite extraordinary. Where would we be without our local proprietors: the eco-friendly organic family farm produce stands, early rising dairy farmers, cheese artisans, nocturnal delivery trucks brimming with fresh grocery produce, our dentists who nag at us to floss, our dedicated estate planners and insurance advisors, the smiling family-owned jeweler, the local spirits merchants who sell the red wine that keeps your cholesterol ratio in check, the trusted family physicians, and the neighborhood health clubs where we take a *schvitz*—sweat—and schmooze with supportive friends of like interests. They all affect our family's health. Even the relentless teasing from the gang at the party supply company keeps me in stitches with their bad puns and jokes. Laughter is outstanding medicine. Hearty laughter gives our lungs and hearts a workout, strengthens our immune systems, and may help lower blood pressure. In this crazy, stressful, beautiful world, it's vitally relevant that we nurture our sense of humor and personal integrity and back away from engaging in anything that waters down our sense of community.

Finally, who doesn't want to identify with the winning, excitement, entertainment, and pride offered by powerfully built, role model thoroughbreds who play professional sports? The teamwork and pride of participating in special community sports programs or attending a professional basketball game is powerful primal therapy: stress relief. *Cheer, scream, shout, and let it all out!*

This is the proud community of which I effuse. Each of them is a part of me. Together we succeed. Identify, acknowledge, and treasure yours, and maximize your awareness and patronize their contributions. They are the lifeblood of your family and village, the main ingredients in the tasty, nutritious casserole of life. Bon appetite!

Locally and globally, we are all the ingredients of a large community casserole. All thriving, living beings existing in a well-seasoned, structured, supportive community simmered to perfection for the good of the whole. Our families' glowing health is a teeny-weeny part of that success, but that success is a vital part of our vibrantly healthy, supportive village.

I wish to express my appreciation to members of my community who supported me in the publication of *The Dawning of the Age of Asparagus: Give Peas a Chance!*

The Indiana Pacers
Good Earth Whole Foods
Indianapolis Fruit Company
Cash and Carry Paper Company
Cabot Creamery (Vermont)
National Institute for Fitness and Sport
Northwestern Mutual Financial Services

Pedigo Jewelers
Indiana Organics Council
Karen Fischer, D.D.S.

Eco-foods
Essays and Editorials

Creator, open our hearts
   to peace and healing between all people.
Creator, open our hearts
   to provide and protect for all children of the earth.
Creator, open our hearts
   to end exclusion, violence, and fear among all.
Thank-you for the gifts of this day and every day.

—Alycia Longriver (Native American) 1995

Live Long and Prosper

There are countless folks freaking out over environmentally caused diseases who are seeking ways to maximize their health. A properly functioning immune system seems to be more relevant than ever in our lifetime—especially for our children and elders whose immune systems aren't so strong. Could food be the answer?

Lurking around every corner in the grocery aisles is another popular diet du jour product waiting to leap off the shelf and into your shopping basket, which, ideally, should contain only a variety of fresh, unprocessed, nutrient-rich, healing foods.

Fad diets are nothing more than band-aid cop-outs. I believe the solution lies in working together as a family, avoiding processed junk foods, changing your culinary paradigm, and becoming happy, healthy, energetic, conscious eaters who incorporate variety, balance, and moderation into your diets. How you feel at this very moment in time is profoundly affected by your previous meal. Your mood is in the food.

Most nutritionists will assert that dieting per se doesn't work, since dieting requires constant obsessing and fretting over which foods to feed yourself and your family. The secret to healthy eating lies in turning food preparation into family fun, generously seasoned with daily, educated lifestyle choices and prudent shopping selections. Our children and grandchildren desperately need good role models for healthy lifestyles, and what we learn about food we learn as children.

I grew up in typical Midwestern fashion, where at the dining table meat and potatoes ruled and gravy was a beverage. Abruptly, in 1988, my self-destructive lifestyle changed when a cardiologist told me I was either going to die or need a new ticker. Believe me, the prospect of death can be really motivating, so I took my first baby step toward a higher quality of life. So long, fried chicken, beer, and cigarettes, and hello to a membership to the local gym.

Over the years, I have become so much of a vegetarian that I lean toward the sunlight. But I didn't become vegetarian overnight. I know that if food isn't pleasing to the eye and nose, as well as the taste buds, no one will eat it. Therefore, I try to cover all the bases of eating wisely when I lecture and write, and my simple-to-prepare recipes that I have developed over the years have been proven to appeal to a wide variety of palates.

Americans seem confused about what should be one of life's essential pleasures: dining. We're unclear about what to eat, how much to eat, and the contents and safety of our food. According to the American Dietetic Association, 85 percent of consumers say nutrition is important. Another 38 percent have made their diets more healthful, and 65 percent of people are concerned about obesity. Chemically and genetically altered "Frankenfoods" are becoming more universally disdained. Man cannot improve on God's work.

Sadly, most Americans seem to be addicted to convenience. In a time-strapped, supersized world, many of us mindlessly overeat all the wrong foods. We eat simply for the sake of eating, living to eat rather than eating to live. I want to emphasize that food is *not* just something to quiet a rumbling stomach.

I lovingly encourage everyone to look at food as not just nourishment but also as a source of disease prevention. I invite you to discover the pleasure of slow, conscious chewing, savoring each bite. Pause for a moment to give thanks and to appreciate the

seductive aroma and multiple textures of a colorful meal. We need to return to dining together as a family and taking family-bonding after-supper walks where you can relish the comforting, delicious sense of community.

In *The Dawning of the Age of Asparagus,* I emphasize the importance of eating fresh, organic farm produce that is pesticide and insecticide free and unprocessed whole grains in their natural, God-given state. Support your local farming economy!

This book offers a style of eating that will help you on the way to optimal health. It covers everything from soup to nuts, and contains recipes calling for easy-to-find ingredients that require the simplest of cooking techniques. No exotic ingredients or high-tech equipment needed here!

Open your mind, as well as your mouth, and get ready to enjoy these simple recipes that I have infused with humor, love, and a simple philosophy. Eat to live, give thanks to your Creator, learn, and live well.

Food in the Name of Celebration

A Nutritional Paradox

"Hey, it's Grandpa Milty's birthday. Let's send out for a jumbo, double cheese, pepperoni, and sausage pizza. And, oh, yes, will someone pick up a gooey cake from the grocery, along with that yummy chardonnay he likes?"

Why not just plunge a corkscrew into the old boy's heart?

For as long as I can remember, birthdays, holidays, anniversaries, and other of life's milestones were our culture's green light for indulging in unnatural, chemically treated processed foods that suck our energy, render our bodies toxic, weaken our immune systems, and thwart our mental capacities, all as we eagerly hoist a glass (or five) of alcoholic cheer to toast the occasion, ultimately rendering us brain-dead the next morning. *Happy birthday, Milty! Got any Pepto?*

It pains me to recall that, when I used to take cocktailing to Olympian levels, in order to endure my mind-numbing hangovers, I found paradoxical solace in greasy buckets of Colonel Sanders gizzards, creamy coleslaw, and packages of sugar-glazed dunkin' sticks. Thinking back on those days, it's a miracle indeed that I recovered from terminal heart disease. That was one hundred pounds ago, but who's counting?

Why is it that in the name of tradition and celebration humans rationalize eating, drinking, and snacking on such quantities of "forbidden" foods: artfully decorated cakes loaded with sugar; thick, cheesy pizzas and greasy meats; eggnog and ice cream; cookies washed down with quarts of sugary, carbonated soft drinks; and, often, too many cocktails. And let's not forget succulent, nitrate-laced hot dogs and sumptuous, chargrilled, super-sized, cow burgers. Last year, at my granddaughter Morgan's birthday party, we were all blue-lipped after shoveling down birthday cake with an inch-thick coating of electric blue icing. Hours later, after a trip to the washroom, I remember wondering, "When did I eat blue corn?"

Are Americans trading their lives for a moment of instant gratification? Yes! It's a stressful world, and we want to feel good. For many of us, when we are stressed, depressed, or want to celebrate, we turn to food and beverage, our best buddies.

Consider this artery-clogging example of gluttony: According to the *Nutrition Action Health Letter*, Pizza Hut's "Big New Yorker" weighs in at three pounds prior to baking. Even if you split this monster with three other people, you'll end up with 760 meaningless calories, a full day's quota of saturated fat (18 g), and an artery-detonating 2,280 mg of sodium. Next time, celebrate with a Healthy Choice Supreme French Bread Pizza and you'll take in a scant 330 calories, 1.5 grams of fat, and 580 mg of sodium. Now that's something we can celebrate in good conscience!

My daughter Tiffany sincerely wants her family to eat better, but protests to me that grocery store shelves are loaded with foods that are overly processed and over the top with sugar and hydrogenated fats. In fact, Tiff tells me she gets the bulk of her cardiovascular exercise by cruising aisle after aisle at the market, wearing out her tennies hunting and gathering fresh, wholesome foods for her family. "It's a dangerous place, a grocery store," she tells me, "with eye-catching, circus-like mountains of candy, cereals, junky albeit seductive and attractively colored packages, all screaming 'if you want to be hip, buy me!'"

Before you reach for that bright box full of empty calories, keep in mind that it's the goal of greedy ad agency types to convince us

what we should eat and what is hip. Learn, as a family, how to think for yourselves. For example, do you think your dog cares whether Gravy Train makes it's own gravy?

Bottom-line driven grocers profit by positioning what they want most to sell at eye level, while placing the healthier selections, like whole wheat crackers, sea salt, or expeller pressed oils, on the lower shelves around your ankles. When I was a naïve twenty-something working in various North Shore seafood restaurants and Boston delicatessens, the kindly old deli men explained it to me. "Wendelleh," they'd say, "eye appeal is buy appeal, and eye level is buy level."

Since then, I snicker every time I go through the grocery checkout. They were right. My suggestion: Politely urge the grocery store managers to provide healthier alternatives and move them higher up on the shelves. But if the grocery store manager is overweight, I wager all you'll get is an incredulous look.

CHANGE THE GAME PLAN AND EAT SMARTER!

First, grasp the reality of your intentions. For example, after a recent observation of the annual Halloween glucose field day, my wife, Sandi, and I looked at each other and said, "Yikes!" We shook our heads, aghast at the amount of sugary, toxic waste we had handed out to the neighborhood children in the name of tradition. Perhaps next Halloween we'll atone by encouraging one of our grandchildren to dress up as a distressed pancreas and collect for the American Diabetic Association.

Go for color and variety. Take the kids to the grocery and introduce them to "Roy G. Biv" (**R**ed, **O**range, **Y**ellow, **G**reen, **B**lue, **I**ndigo, and **V**iolet). Try comparing vegetables to the colors of the rainbow. Make selecting healthy food fun for the kids by taking them for an educational stroll through the produce aisle before you let them drag you to the candy section. Tell them that colorful

plant foods are diamonds and that they are the jewelers. This way, when their teachers ask where vegetables and fruits come from, your kids won't say, "The grocery store." When your children become adults, they will *not* willingly eat what they were *not* offered as youngsters. Studies show eight to fifteen exposures are needed to gain acceptance of new foods.

Unless you've been living under a pile of rock candy, we can all agree that eating more plant foods has miraculous health benefits. Eating more plant foods helps cut your family's intake of animal foods, which, when eaten in supersized quantities, are linked to a whole bunch of degenerative diseases.

Rock the house! Add a variety of taste, texture, excitement, and color to your next celebration by encouraging everyone to experiment with new foods and new combinations. Aesthetically arranged fruit and vegetable trays, turkey breast wraps, and low-fat chips are several ways to add health to a celebration. Produce provides key vitamins and minerals, not to mention some wonderful taste experiences. So, try avocado on your turkey burger, or assemble a pretty bowl of yogurt, garnish it with fresh fruit, and serve it over angel food cake. And what ever happened to homemade popcorn, as opposed to the microwave versions full of trans-fats?

We're missing the opportunity to create a memory and share a legacy of togetherness. I remember my siblings and me standing at the stove, each excitedly taking his turn shaking the popcorn popper until the last kernel exploded before dousing the hot corn with gobs of butter and hunkering down in front of the TV to watch Ed Sullivan, with all of us nibbling out of the same wooden bowl together. Not Ed, just us. Do you remember doing things like that? Revisit your childhood with your own children. Not only will you help them make new discoveries, but you'll also increase their motivation by realizing that celebratory meals can be adventurous, fun, healing, and delicious. (Of course, replace the butter on the popcorn with olive oil or a non-trans fat margarine, please!)

Add power foods to the celebration menu such as peanut butter and jelly sammies made with organic peanut butter from the whole foods store, or Smuckers Natural peanut butter. Consider no-sugar-added jams, bean dips, turkey wraps with shredded veggies, oatmeal cookies, reduced-fat cheese, sorbet, watermelon wedges, blueberries in low-fat sour cream, apples slices spread with peanut butter, turkey chili, and deviled eggs made with reduced-fat mayonnaise. Or how about hummus with whole wheat pita bread, pretzels with mustard, homemade whole wheat pizza, and brown rice cakes with slices of low-fat cheese topped with salsa? Just think small and kick the vending machine mentality. You're smarter than that.

Instead of trying to win the family popularity contest, why not use celebrations to educate and glorify life and nature rather than to reinforce negative behavior, perpetuating degenerative disease. Tradition, thy name is stubbornness. It's got to change someday—it must.

Teaching An Old Dog
New Tricks

It's Never Too Late To Go Vegetarian

The beef industry has contributed to more American deaths than all the wars of the century, all natural disasters, and all automobile accidents combined. If beef is your idea of "real food for real people," you'd better live real close to a real good hospital.

—Neal D. Barnard, M.D.,
president, Physicians Committee
for Responsible Medicine

I really dig growing older, don't you?

Where we used to fight for our right to party, we now fight for our right to age, take naps, and wrinkle with dignity. No one needs to remind us that as we age, our bodies become less forgiving.

Now that we're, ahem, "older," we're likely feeling confident that we've lived the first half of our lives acquiring the knowledge that will usher us gracefully into our twilight years.

We boomers take umbrage with aging stereotypes and old rules; we choose to age with style. Boomers prefer to stay challenged, to contribute, and keep learning. The old adage that "you can't teach an old dog new tricks" isn't true even about dogs, and it clearly isn't true about people. We're never too young or old to combat disease and the signs of aging, so forget about that aging gracefully

crap—it's a cop-out. We can undo a lot of damage by consuming an eco-friendly, vegetarian diet. I'm serious! Our Earth Suits were created with a rather prodigious ability to heal themselves, if the damage is not too great.

Our ripening creeps unexpectedly and silently upon us, and there's no escaping the fact that we're all growing one year older every three hundred and sixty-five days. Science tells us we can take preventive measures by eating right now, keeping active, and drinking plenty of clean water. In addition, we're learning we can significantly reduce our chances of needless potential damage to our Earth Suits by going veggie.

Need more convincing? Consider this: How we perceive ourselves aging usually depends upon our age. By the time we reach the ripe old age of forty, we're already obsessing on methods to reverse, slow, or delay the aging process. We exercise; we shop for healthier foods, toss back handfuls of colorful, expensive, vitamins, and buy youthful clothing and expensive facial creams. While these steps are useful and can have some desirable effects, they don't provide a feasible long-term strategy.

According to the American Dietetic Association and the Dietitians of Canada, "A well-planned vegetarian diet can be a healthful alternative to meat-based meals for all age groups, including older adults." Scientific research supports this statement, demonstrating that eating a wide variety of fruits, vegetables, and fibrous foods, and less animal protein, can lower blood pressure, diminish the risk of heart attack and stroke, and improve your sense of humor. Pass the edamame, please!

When I was but a freckle-faced lad fidgeting through Sunday morning church service, the droning of the minister and the ensuing boredom often encouraged me to gaze around and check out everyone else. *Gee, I sure hope I don't look like that when I get old! What a prune-neck,* I would muse. At fifteen, aging was inconceivable, but ironically, now I'm a prune neck too. Every now and then, as if the minister seemed to know that I (and likely several others) was daydreaming, he'd jolt us out of our seats, bellowing, "Your body is a holy temple of God. Do not defile it with smoke or drink!"

That was it, I thought. We're all going straight to hell! Do not pass Go, do not collect two hundred dollars. Personally, I have a hard time accepting health tips from an overweight, pipe-smoking clergyman or doctor, so I disregarded the minister's warning and ate and drank whatever I wanted, with no thought for tomorrow.

I was due for a pretty ugly wake-up call, though. Fourteen years and one hundred pounds ago, I was going to die from viral heart disease. I knew I had to change my behavior, and I converted to vegetarianism. As a result, my health has never been better. It's human nature to gamble and wait until we smack the wall before affecting healthy changes in our diet and lifestyle. Sort of like a game of chicken with death. I'm proud that I kicked death's ugly butt with natural vegetarian food and a positive attitude.

OLD DOGS AND HEALTHY NEW TRICKS

Whether you're in your thirties, forties, fifties, sixties, or older, becoming a vegetarian can be relatively easy, and its health benefits make it highly rewarding. It's primarily a behavioral mindset, but it requires a gradual process. You can't just get up one morning and casually decide, "Hey, I think I'll become a vegetarian today." It doesn't work that way. You've been following certain dietary practices for a number of decades now, and your Earth Suit needs time to adjust to each culinary addition and deletion. It's a psycho-physiological and biochemical evolution that must be researched and approached with patience. Our carbon-based bodies need time to adjust to nutritional alterations.

The first step toward vegetarianism should involve gradually

cutting back on fatty red meats, deep-fried anything, and junk foods and increasing your intake of organic fruits and vegetables, and yogurt. Make your changes gradually, practice and accept them, and then lovingly embrace them. Hold your ground and keep reminding yourself that you enjoy the taste of life more than the taste of beef.

After about a month, advance to other changes such as eliminating white foods (white rice, flour, bread, baked/mashed potatoes, and cream sauces) and gradually substituting brown rice and other whole grains, nuts, unprocessed soybean products, satisfyingly chewy and flavorful whole-grain breads, protein- and fiber-loaded legumes, and some granolas (read the labels on those, though). We need those complex carbohydrates!

As we age, our vitamin needs also change. As a new vegetarian, you need to be especially aware of B complex vitamins. I recommend a liquid, sublingual (under the tongue) B-complex for optimum absorption. Get more antioxidants and beta carotene by eating carrots, apricots, red peppers, and yellow summer squash. Vitamin C, needed for cell protection, you can get by munching oranges, kiwi, and peppers. Vitamin E, another antioxidant that is believed to help slow the aging process, can be found in cold-pressed vegetables oils, raw nuts, and seeds. The antoxidant properties of selenium protects against ultraviolet-induced cell damage and helps keep skin elastic. Good food sources for selenium include supplements, garlic, onions, and broccoli.

And always, drink plenty of fresh, filtered water and green tea.

As with any other major lifestyle change, before becoming a vegetarian, you should consult your physician. However, most physicians aren't thoroughly trained in nutrition, so you should also consider consulting a vegetarian nutritionist. Above all, don't cave into "magic" diet pills or any of the fad diets so popular today. Eating badly is easy; eating healthily takes focused effort and resolve.

USE IT OR LOSE IT

Sitting around with a shawl around your shoulders and gumming a cream-filled cupcake griping "I'm too old to exercise" is a pile of meadow muffins. It's mind over rocker.

According to a recent U.S. Department of Health and Human Services study, between 28 and 34 percent of adults aged sixty-five to seventy-four and 35 to 44 percent of adults seventy-five and older are inactive, meaning they report no leisure-time moderate activity. Less than a third of Americans in those age ranges exercise twice weekly. Despite the overwhelming number of both private and public gyms, the numbers aren't improving. It's a microcosm of a much larger national problem.

Instead of complaining, try an alternative: a change in behavior. Perceive the inevitable changes brought on by age as problems to be solved, not a fate to be accepted like being dealt a bad hand in poker. Identifying your behavioral shortcomings is the most logical approach, and it provides an honest appraisal of the lifestyle changes that need modification.

For instance, you could say to yourself, "Put that bowl of ice cream back in the freezer, you old dog, and have some organic vanilla yogurt instead." Then after that, take a walk with the grandkids, and learn some new tricks. Woof!

In summary, the solution to healthy and vigorous old age is to eat to live in harmony with nature, and keep those creaking old bones and muscles moving. It is only in doing that you experience consequences, and *it is the consequences of doing well that leads to a fuller, more enjoyable life.*

Your worst-case scenario would be to lie in bed and die of nothing worse than a very active and happy old age. Actually, going to bed and waking up dead sounds like a winner. Beats the hell out of late-life morbidity.

Move over, Rover, and let the veggies take over.

Asparagus Tips

"In the spring, a young man's fancy lightly turns to thoughts of love." Or was that asparagus to which Sir Alfred Lord Tennyson was alluding?

As the brown-gray mood of winter gives way to warmer temperatures, crocuses, chirping robins, butterflies, bright green grass, and budding trees, spring brings forth life, robustly rising through the brown, hardened winter soil. And Mother Nature's ultimate finger food, asparagus, eagerly pokes their purple tips through the soil, as if anticipating the warmth of summer to come.

The word asparagus is derived from the Greek word, *asparago,* meaning "to sprout" or "shoot up," and first appeared in English print around 1000 A.D. This revered, luxurious member of the lily family, which historically was reserved for royalty and rulers, is originally native to the eastern Mediterranean and Asia Minor. Way back in 200 B.C., Cato the Elder reportedly documented detailed growing instructions. The Egyptians began cultivating it, and at that time, self-respecting Romans from Pliny to Julius Caesar coveted the delectable spear. In fact, Roman emperors were so terribly fond of asparagus that they kept a special fleet of ships solely to fetch it.

Ancient Romans hoarded private stashes of asparagus because, besides its seductive flavor, they believed it was a cure for all ailments, which is conclusive evidence of man's recognition of food as medicine. *Hippocrates was right!*

Nutritional Benefits

Did you know that asparagus is one of the most nutritional, well-balanced veggies in existence? Well, now you do, and here's why:

- A five-ounce portion of asparagus provides 60 percent of the recommended daily allowance for folacin, which is necessary for blood cell formation. Folic acid also aids in the prevention of liver disease, heart disease, amd cervical, colon, and rectal cancers.

- Asparagus is low in calories, only about twenty per each five-ounce serving, which equates to less than four calories per spear.

- Asparagus is a good source of potassium, which helps regulate the electrolyte balance within cells and helps maintain normal heart function and blood pressure.

- The crisp little spear also contains fiber, thiamin, and vitamin B6, and is one of the richest sources of rutin, a phytochemical/drug that strengthens capillary walls.

- Asparagus is especially rich in antioxidant nutrients. Vitamins A, C, and E are amply represented.

- Among the well-known virtues of the medicinal action of asparagus are its diuretic and laxative effects. It's been found to be beneficial for those who are sedentary and suffer from gravel and dropsy.

- Asparagus contains steroids that mimic pheromones, which purportedly make you attractive to lovers. In nineteenth-century France, bridegrooms were required to eat several courses of asparagus because of its alleged powers for enhancing arousal.

In an article, Gordon Wardlaw, Ph.D., R.D., Associate Professor of Medical Dietetics Division at Ohio State University, stated that

asparagus provides more to a meal than you might think. As most of the population already know, a diet rich in phytonutrients (*phyto* is the Greek word for plants) found in fruits and vegetables can slow the development of cancer and heart disease. Most impressive, a chemical compound called glutathione has garnered the center of the plate spotlight in nutrition research.

Asparagus contains more glutathione than all other fruits and vegetables researched to date. Grab a spear and savor what this unique phytochemical can offer your family at the next meal.

- It participates in a process, which cells use to break down highly toxic peroxide and other high-energy, oxygen-rich compounds, in turn preventing them from destroying cell membranes, genetic materials (DNA), and other cell constituents. Glutathione also participates in repair of damaged DNA.
- It can bind carcinogens in the body, aiding in their removal via the urine and feces.
- It stimulates immune function.
- And, it can recycle vitamins C and E back to their active forms. In this way, it is easy to see that glutathione may help reduce cataract development in the eye.

Ancient Chinese herbalists have used asparagus root for centuries. The root contains compounds called steroidal glycosides, which may have anti-inflammatory properties to ease the pain of arthritis-related conditions. In 1991, an Italian researcher reported a compound found in asparagus that had shown some antiviral activity in test-tube studies.

If you grow your own, the Michigan Asparagus Advisory Board shared some interesting facts with me regarding the process. Asparagus spears grow from a crown that is planted about a foot deep in sandy soils, and under ideal conditions, a spear can grow ten inches in a twenty-four-hour period. Each crown will send spears up for about six to seven weeks during spring and early

summer. The outdoor temperature will determine how much time will occur between each picking. Early in the season, there may be four to five days between pickings, and as the days and nights get warmer, a particular patch may have to be picked every twenty-four hours. *Oh, boy!*

The advisory board added that after the harvest is done, the plants grow into ferns, which produce red berries and the nutrients necessary for a healthy and productive crop the next season. Be patient. An asparagus planting is usually not harvested for the first three years after the crowns are planted, thus allowing the crown to develop a strong, fibrous root system. Your patience will be rewarded for years to come, for a well cared-for asparagus plant will generally produce for about fifteen years.

THIS BUD'S FOR YOU

Asparagus is not cheap, especially in winter, so selecting, storing, and cooking the vegetable becomes especially relevant.

Because not all conventional grocery stores carry the freshest asparagus, you must learn how to recognize its freshness and quality before you make your wallet-busting investment.

Taking care not to get busted by the "produce cops," select an asparagus stalk from a bunch that is firm and has tightly closed buds, and gently bend the stalk to check for crispness.

The thickness of the stalks makes no difference; however, most aficionados will agree the larger the diameter, the better the quality. The color should be bright green with subtle hints of purple. Discoloration and fading indicates that it is not fresh, and you should gently inform the produce manager.

I have discovered the best way to store asparagus spears in the refrigerator is to place them upright in a jar or bowl with an inch or so of water, just like you'd place flowers in a vase. This method will keep asparagus fresh for about a week and keep it from

becoming rubbery, dehydrated, and ultimately discarded after a few days in your crisper drawer. How dare you treat the king of vegetables any other way?

COOKING AND STORING

Asparagus should still be rigid and crisp after cooking, so if yours goes limp, you've blown it. Asparagus can be steamed, sautéed in olive oil, or lightly grilled, which is my personal favorite. Anyone who overcooks it deserves a good flogging. And in a boiling steamer basket, one can rapidly turn crisp asparagus into mush. Pay attention. "As quick as cooking asparagus" was an old Roman saying meaning something had to be accomplished rapidly. When you insert a knifepoint in the thickest part and encounter no resistance, they are done and need to be quickly shocked in an ice-water bath to maintain brilliant green color and stop the cooking.

Prepare asparagus for cooking by breaking off the bottom woody pulpy stem. If your feel it's necessary, which it is not, peel the lower part of the stalks with a potato peeler.

Rub the washed and towel-dried spears with a little olive oil, dust with some salt and pepper, and grill on two sides for no more than 2 minutes. (That's one minute per side.) My wife, Sandi, and I add the grilled spears to a traditional crudités of spring vegetables along with halved, grilled baby reds or Yukon golds to add variety. First, parboil the potatoes, drain well, toss in olive oil, salt and pepper, then grill over medium fire (not open flame) until grill lines form and the spud becomes a golden brown. Crunchy, smoky, delicious, and unique!

To steam, place whole, trimmed asparagus on a steamer rack over rapidly boiling water. Cover the pan and start timing—five to eight minutes, depending on the girth and length of the asparagus.

You can liven up the asparagus by topping it with a little squeeze of lemon juice after cooking; top it with yogurt, low-fat

mayonnaise, or nonfat sour cream; or drizzle it with olive oil infused with herbs such as chives, chervil, parsley, savory, or tarragon. Finally, compliment the asparagus with a lovely glass of chenin blanc, fume blanc, or French colombard. *Ooh-la-la!*

Personally, I think you can't improve on asparagus except to add a smidgen of salt to bring out its natural sweetness. So lose that yellow gravy of hollandaise and butter. You can live without it—and a lot longer, I might add.

FINGERS VS. THE FORK

Celebrate spring and the beginning of summer by harvesting a basket of fresh asparagus, whether from your family garden, community organic farmers roadside markets or the ubiquitous conventional grocery stores. But, what *is* the socially or politically correct way to eat and enjoy asparagus?

Once, several years ago, Sandi and I were in West Palm Beach as guests at the home of very dear friends. The table was elaborately appointed with fine crystal, bone china, Irish linen, flowers, and deeply tanned guests dripping with precious stones and Versace gowns. The menu: grilled salmon filet, new red potatoes with garlic and rosemary, blanched fresh asparagus, and some esoteric white Bordeaux. To our astonishment, everyone began eating the asparagus with their fingers. Well, when in Rome, do as the Romans. Later on, after some investigation, we discovered that it was socially acceptable to eat asparagus with one's fingers, even as my neighbor Kathy remarked, when, during a church social, she was remonstrated for doing so. Apparently we've been living under a rock. *Freedom from asparagus oppression!*

And while we're discussing manners, may I touch on a somewhat delicate issue? It's not uncommon for many (somewhere between 20 to 40 percent of the population) to note an oddly pungent odor to their urine after eating asparagus. Not to worry.

That odor is caused by the sulfur compounds in the spring vegetable. Evidently, another culprit, a chemical compound called methanethiol, also shares the blame. It is famous for its odiferousness in rotten eggs, cabbages and paper mills.

As you can see, asparagus has always been in my life even from childhood when Mom used to open a can and make us all gag and screech in horror. But when Mom began growing it and cooking it correctly, our opinion changed immediately. If you've grown up eating asparagus out of a tin can, then it cannot be said you have truly experienced the ritual taste of spring.

I'll never forget Mom's warning as my brothers and I ran through the family garden, uprooting and using asparagus spears as swords in our imaginary swashbuckling fantasy: "Don't run with asparagus in your hand. You'll poke someone's eye out!"

Breakfast

Jᴜᴍᴘsᴛᴀʀᴛ Yᴏᴜʀ Bʀᴀɪɴ

The day breaks: the smell of coffee and simmering sausage, the gentle sound of feet padding. Yawning, the family stumbles into the kitchen bleary-eyed, proclaiming the mantra of the new millennium: "No time to eat, gotta run, I'll be late." Plus your significant other has slipped out the door and spaced out eating altogether. What, no "good morning"?

Not the best way to start the day off in the pink.

If you keep forgetting to eat breakfast, or kiss your wife good morning, as sure as the sun's gonna shine, it is because you really *need* to eat breakfast.

Breakfast around our house as we grew up was a special time. School-teacher Mom always set the table the night before, so in the morning we'd sit down and say grace over a hot bowl of Cream of Wheat and glasses of juice and whole milk, and discuss the day and be interrogated on whether we had completed our homework. We looked forward to what Mom prepared and the quality time spent together talking, sharing news, and just being a family.

Over the years we've had beaten into our heads with a dried-out waffle the adage that "breakfast is the most important meal of the day." Now, if you will cease reading the side panel of your cereal box long enough, I will attempt to explain why that is true.

"Breaking the fast" is exactly what the term "breakfast" implies. Let's face it—eight hours without food is a long time. Glucose levels drop, and since the brain itself possesses no reserves of glucose, its main energy source, glucose must constantly be replenished.

Even short-term hunger from avoiding breakfast may dramatically decrease your attention span and ability to focus and concentrate. Sound familiar?

Don't blame late-night TV or that last glass of wine for your yawning and fighting to stay awake around ten o'clock each morning. It is a direct result of what you did or didn't eat for breakfast and how your body is responding to it, especially if you had "dessert" for breakfast. Did you? If so, the oxygen your brain needs is in your stomach, aiding in the digestion of that sugary butter-bomb you had for breakfast. As a result, you're crashing from the sugar buzz.

"When you consider it's been eight or nine hours since you've had a meal, it's obvious that refueling at breakfast will make you feel and perform better during the day," says Diane Odland, a nutritionist at the U.S. Department of Agriculture Food and Nutrition Center. Studies have shown that eating a healthy breakfast is associated with improved strength and endurance in the late morning, along with a better attitude toward office or housework. Further studies have indicated that sustained mental work requires a large turnover of brain glucose and its metabolic components.

In today's rushed, time-strapped society, a nutritionally sound breakfast takes a back seat to busy schedules. All too often it ends up being taken care of by the nearest fast-food death trap or a can of cola, especially with those cheery "non-morning" people who would love to avoid that part of the day and everything that comes with it.

Thirty percent of Americans eat breakfast outside of the home. *That must get kind of chilly during the winter!* And that's too bad, since breakfast also provides an excellent opportunity for families

to talk, interact, and bond with each other. Breakfast also offers a perfect opportunity for parentals to serve as family role models for healthy eating habits.

When I was a child, besides the above-mentioned Cream of Wheat, breakfast often consisted of a variety of foods: eggs fried in bacon grease, white bread, ham steak, sausage patties, breakfast casseroles, French toast, Aunt Jemima, sugary cold cereals, and, if we behaved, Dad would buy us doughnuts—jelly filled, cake, or yeast, still warm from the local Irvington bakery. In the blissful 1950s, we didn't look upon those greasy, sugary shortening-based pastries as breakfast desserts but rewards. We simply and innocently didn't know any better, but that is exactly what they were: desserts.

It is the sugars in these foods that zap you and have you tired out by mid-morning. *Zoom, crash, and burn!* It's a vicious cycle that requires you to take another "hit" of sugar to give you the lift you need to make it through the day.

Nowadays, I avoid processed sugar and begin my day either with whole-grain granola with fruit and soymilk or several slices of heavily grained bread with olive oil, and a piece of fruit mid-morning. At all costs I avoid the heavy, greasy foods that are difficult for our Earth Suits to digest, and which would tire me out and render me a mental vegetable—a state for which I need no encouragement.

In modern America, advertising campaigns enthusiastically endorse the "grab and go" breakfasts consisting of 2,000-calorie cinnamon buns, greasy sausage gravy and biscuits, deep-fried hash browns, buttery muffins, hand-held breakfast burritos, bagels with gobs of cream cheese, and belly-busting biscuits bursting with the cholesterol triad of cheese, meat, and eggs. And all this is chased down with a "nourishing" can of soda, the opiate of the media manipulated masses.

The devastating results? Altered health, memory, thinking, and performance.

In today's society, we need to stay mentally sharp in order to

succeed in business or run a household and keep a leg-up on the competition, not the couch. Remember this: Whether or not you *have* breakfast—and 83 percent of us do—matters less than *what* you have. Just eat!

WHAT SHOULD WE EAT FOR BREAKFAST?

Base your breakfast on foods that are ready to eat or take little preparation time: organic yogurt, whole wheat pancakes, instant grits, Cream of Wheat, muesli, oatmeal, granola, and sugar-free, fortified, fibrous cold cereals, fresh or frozen fruits, whole-grain toast, sugar-free jams and preserves, fruit smoothies, carrot juice, bran muffins, cottage cheese, Egg Beaters, turkey bacon, or soy sausage. Try cutting down on whole milk by switching to 2 percent or fortified vanilla soymilk. Soy milk over granola is a naturally delicious combination as well as granola and yogurt mixed together, which I refer to as the "French depth-charge." A very satisfying, filling and nutritious breakfast.

If you're just not hungry, at least drink some fresh juice. Something is better than nothing.

Need to eat on the go? Try assembling celery stuffed with peanut butter (organic and trans-fat free preferred) or soy butter, dried fruits, or any of the organic vegetable juices you see sprouting up at grocery stores.

And here is some interesting news. Do not skip breakfast if you're on a diet. Evidently there is no science to support that skipping meals will help you lose weight. In fact, studies show that most people who skip breakfast tend to eat *more* later in the day and select more calorically dense foods than those who eat breakfast, according to the International Food Information Council Federation.

Data from a U.S.D.A. study grouped adults according to their breakfast eating habits:

- 22 percent ate bread, bagels, English muffins, or similar items (without eggs or cereal)
- 17 percent ate cold cereal (without eggs)
- 15 percent ate eggs (with or without bacon, toast, cereal, or other foods)
- 15 percent ate pastries (like doughnuts) and/or coffee or a soft drink
- 6 percent ate just fruit or juice
- 4 percent are hot cereal
- 17 percent ate nothing at all

The study also looked at what each group consumed throughout the day, and the egg eaters and pastry and/or coffee-eaters did the worst. They consumed the most saturated fat and the least fiber. On the other hand, those who ate cereals or fruit ate less saturated fat than the others. Cold cereal eaters also got the most iron and folate.

So arise and smell the green tea! It is never to late to wake up to a healthy start.

Take Two Apples and Call Me In the Morning

GETTING TO THE CORE OF THE MATTER

When you really think about it, the first real commandment in the Bible was Eve firmly telling her new husband, "Adam? Eat this apple . . . now!"

"Yes, dear." Precedent established.

Apparently, she was having a devil of a time tempting Adam, Cain, and Abel to eat their fruits and vegetables. Some things never change, do they?

Since the beginning of the peopling of our planet, the apple has emerged as a celebrated fruit. In ancient Greek and Roman mythology, the apple is referred to as a symbol of love and beauty. Cleopatra was rumored to have placed an apple in Caesar's chariot lunch box every day before he went into battle. The ancient Romans highly prized apple trees and their fruit. Evidently reluctant to do without them, when they conquered England in the first century B.C. it is believed they took apple trees with them.

In turn, the English took apples with them when they sailed west to the New World. According to the Internet Broadcasting System, "about 1629, both the seeds and the trees were brought to America. John Endicott, one of the early governors of Massachusetts Bay Colony, is said to have brought the first trees to America. John Chapman, also helped to encourage apple growing as

he carried apple seeds with him wherever he went, and planted them in thinly settled parts of the country." Enter, Johnny Appleseed.

In modern-day America, the apple remains king on every lunch box and fruit basket manifest.

Assigned the ironic moniker "forbidden fruit," apples nevertheless can assist in preventing cancer, heart disease, and strokes, as well as promoting healthy lungs, weight loss, good dental health, and the reduction of serum cholesterol in our arteries. As you can see, apples can keep your family healthy.

What exactly is in an apple?

The average nineteen pounds of apples each American consumes annually contain between 80 to 85 percent kidney-flushing water. Despite the large proportion of water, though, apples are rich in vitamins. And, "Arrrrr, matey," if you ever get scurvy; they are the most valuable cure, since apples contain vitamin C, an antioxidant, which also exerts positive effects on the cardiovascular system. French researchers indicate that apples render vitamin C more available to blood and organs, thus helping vitamin C from other sources go farther.

Orchards of studies have shown that a diet containing lots of apples does indeed reduce blood cholesterol levels, with special thanks to the phytonutrients within the fruit and skin.

Choke on this, die-hard smokers, and please pay particular attention: The National Cancer Institute has reported that foods containing flavonoids, a class of antioxidants like those found in apples, may actually reduce the risk of lung cancer by as much as 50 percent. Not too long ago, a very dear friend unexpectedly and sadly passed away from advanced lung cancer, even though she never smoked. Need I say more?

A Cornell University study indicated phytochemicals in the skin

or flesh of an apple inhibited the reproduction of colon cancer cells by 43 percent. Don't you wish you could say the same about—*gag, shudder!*—chicken skin? The apple's skin contains about 4 milligrams of quercetin, an antioxidant that prevents oxygen molecules from damaging individual cells, which can lead to cancer. A 2001 Mayo Clinic study indicated that quercetin, a flavonoid abundant in apples, helps prevent the growth of prostate cancer cells.

To peel or not to peel—not so appealing

Most Americans will agree the meat of the apple is the most delicious, but the skin definitely has the most nutrition. Just think of all the time you'll save peeling those tart Granny Smiths for that next deep-dish apple pie.

Don't throw the baby out with the bathwater

Do you recall in 1989 when CBS's *60 Minutes* announced to America the since-unsubstantiated claims that the pesticide Alar posed a serious health threat to young children? That report led some school districts to remove apples from their school programs and unnecessarily freaked out conscientious parents who were trying to develop good eating habits for their kids. The last thing we want is to discourage our precious children and grandkids from eating produce. Do your homework, educate, and be a loving, stalwart roll model.

GETTING TO THE CORE OF A SEEDY ISSUE

If you wish to avoid the controversial waxy coatings applied by most apple producers, which fuse potentially carcinogenic chemicals, such as pesticides, to the outside, simply opt for organically grown apples. They taste so much better. The more you request organic produce, the more your local grocer will accommodate. It's a market-sensitive, bottom-line business; don't be shy about expressing yourself and what you want.

If you think peeling the apple will get rid of the pesticides, you're correct. But remember that you're also peeling away those healthy nutrients. The valuable acids and salt of the apple exist to a special degree in and just below the skin, so to get the full healthy benefit of an apple, it should be consumed as is, in it's original manufacturer packaging.

Bob on this: It's rumored that there is cyanide in apple seeds. *Cyanide?*

Yes, apple seeds contain a substance called amygdalin, the hydrolysis of which can give rise to hydrogen cyanide when the seeds are crushed and moistened. If poisoning is suspected, seek immediate medical treatment, but don't get uptight—you'd have to eat about a bushel at one sitting. Amygdalin commonly occurs not only in apple seeds, but also in the pits of apricots, cherries, and peaches, and in almonds, and is normally not dangerous in itself.

HOW 'BOUT THEM APPLES?

How many do you plan to eat? Eating two or three apples a day engages complex and beneficial physiological processes in the task of reducing blood cholesterol.

It's all about the phytochemical called pectin, a soluble fiber present in most fruits and veggies. Apples contain .78 grams of

pectin per 100 grams of edible fruit, which ranks them fourth in pectin content among the twenty-four common fruits and vegetables tested. Once more, this applies only when one leaves the skin on, which settles that particular debate. Pectin reduces the amount of cholesterol produced in the liver and slows digestion and the rise of blood sugar, making it ideal for diabetics.

COOKING AND HANDLING TIPS

You will notice when you wash conventional waxed apples, a white film will form on the outside. Your guess is as good as mine as to its composition, but it does occur especially when you wash them with dish soap and warm water. I would welcome the opportunity for anyone to explain that one to me. Make it a home experiment with apples and oranges.

Applesauce, by the way, makes a delightful, low-fat baking substitute for fat. Whatever fat or oil the recipe calls for, substitute equal parts applesauce instead. (The one exception is cornbread.) And for a pleasurable "food-gasm," the next time you whip up a fruit smoothie, use freshly squeezed apple cider as your liquid medium. Oh, baby! You'll definitely light up afterward!

APPLE FACTS

* When cooking fresh apples for pies or sauces, the yield is about 50 percent.
* 1 pound raw equals $1/2$ pound cooked.
* Apples absorb odors. They emit ethylene gas, which causes other fruit to ripen quicker.
* Store apples at 35 degrees Fahrenheit and 80 percent humidity to prevent dehydration.

For your Earth Suit to absorb the biggest nutritional bang-for-your-buck, make sure to choose a variety that oxidizes, or turns brown easily, such as Granny Smith. In addition, I gently encourage you to avoid processed apple juice, nor to substitute apple juice for actual apples. The sugary apple juice found in grocery stores contains next to none of the beneficial compounds of potassium, vitamin C, quertecin, and fiber.

If you prefer fresh, seasonal, apple cider from the local orchard, make sure it contains nothing more than pure apple juice. Check with the orchard to guarantee that it takes steps to prevent food-borne illnesses, such as E. coli or salmonella, which can come from contact with animal "gifts" when apples fall on the ground. Some orchards seek the fallen apples because they are sugary ripe and easy to harvest, but those killer pathogens could be lurking.

Michael Jackson once eloquently warbled, "One bad apple don't spoil the whole bunch, girl," but 'tain't so, dudes, 'tain't so!

Chocolate

THE OPIATE OF THE MASSES

Oompah-loompah, doopity do.
Here's some news that you can chew.
Chocolaty chocolate is good for you.

From *Willie Wonka and the Chocolate Factory*

Do you yearn to travel to places like Hershey, Pennsylvania; Cocoa Beach, Florida; or Carmel, California? Welcome to the Chocophile Club.

As I believe a drooling Homer Simpson once so eloquently mused, "Mmmm . . . chocolate!"

For centuries chocolate has mesmerized countless humans as the symbol for love, friendship, and celebration, with its creamy smoothness that melts in our mouths and not in our hands. As a very wise man once said, "If you have melted chocolate on your hands, you're simply not eating it fast enough."

Chocolate, the tasty treat, comes from the cacao (*kah kow*) tree known as *Theobroma cacao*. Pollination of the tree is accomplished by midges, whose wings beat at a thousand times per second, and birds that make their homes in its branches.

The seedpods of this vegetable—that's right, it's a vegetable!—grow on the trunk rather than on the branches, as one might expect. Each pod is the size of a fresh pineapple and holds up to fifty seeds, which is enough to prepare about seven milk chocolate

or two dark chocolate bars. (Hershey's produces over a billion candy bars per year.)

The first people known to have consumed chocolate were the ancient Aztecs of Central America and Mexico. Primarily it was ground, mixed with chiles, and fermented, which turned it into a frothy, bitter, spicy, albeit coveted Mesoamerican luxury beverage. For 90 percent of its history, chocolate was drunk, not eaten. Besides the chiles, the Aztecs also thickened their chocolate drink with cornmeal and sometimes flavored it with honey, vanilla, or flower petals. Sugar, as we know it, was not available at that time. Montezuma was rumored to have exacted his revenge upon his domain by hoarding all the "liquid gold," and it was an honor to be offered a frothy cup from the emperor's private stash. The great emperor was rumored to also have used chocolate to improve his lovemaking.

Hernando Cortez, during his conquest of Mexico, reported that the Aztecs used cocoa beans in the preparation of a beverage, which was reserved for Aztec royalty. Called *chocolati*, which means "cocoa and water," Cortez first savored the treasured liquid when it was served cold in golden goblets at an Aztec banquet in 1519.

Cortez recognized the potential value of the marvelous brown bean and bought a cacao plantation for the sole purpose, as he put it, "To grow money on trees." In those days, chocolate was often referred to as "money on trees," and indeed it was, because a letter written by one Hernando de Oviedo y Valdez told how he was able to purchase a slave for one hundred cacao beans.

Christopher Columbus was wise enough to bring a few of the dark brown almond-shaped beans back with him to Spain, and he presented them to the court of King Ferdinand. In the 1700s, Spain was the first culture to add sugar to the bitter substance, and, remarkably enough, was able to keep the secret from the rest of the world for more than a century.

Nowadays, the future of chocolate is in jeopardy as the cacao tree itself is being threatened by the rainforest deforestation by lumber companies that are harvesting the taller trees that shelter

Give Peas a Chance!

the shade-loving cacao and help maintain the population of midges.

Unfortunately, chocolate also has a dark side that's far from being even semi-sweet. For centuries, the industry has been based on slave labor, and even recently it has been discovered that children are used to harvest the cacao seeds in Africa. Serious steps have been taken to end this practice, however.

Slavery continues to rear its ugly head even now, according to Congressman Eliot L. Engle (D-N.Y.), who is sponsoring an amendment that would require chocolate products to bear labels assuring that no slave labor was used to harvest the cocoa beans used to make them. Knight Ridder found that African boys as young as eleven are sold or tricked into slavery to harvest beans on some of the more than 600,000 cocoa farms in Ivory Coast, the world's leading cocoa producer. "I don't think the American people would want to knowingly eat chocolate or cocoa that was harvested by children who were tricked into slavery," Engle commented.

AN ADDICTIVE TREAT OR DARNED TASTY MEDICINE?

For those of us who feed our souls with chocolate, it comes as great news to discover that this extract of the cacao bean actually has some health benefits. Hallelujah!

Modern studies are showing that the revered cacao bean, first used by the early Olmecs as a medicinal beverage thousands of years ago. The Mayans and Aztec cultures used the beans as currency, and those wealthy enough to have the biggest stash of beans used them to achieve "wisdom and power."

What is it that makes chocolate healthy? The University of California, Davis, has discovered that chocolate contains flavonoids and antioxidants, substances that are good for the heart. Flavonoids, which come from plants, are naturally occurring compounds in the cacao plant, as well as in red wine, tea, and a

variety of fruits and vegetables. Six hours after eating flavonoids, platelet activity and aggregation, responsible for clotting, is reduced. These flavonoids dilate blood vessels, can help improve blood flow to the heart, and act as antioxidants, which help prevent damage caused by free-radical stress.

And finally, flavonoids assist in keeping low-density lipoproteins (LDL), or the bad cholesterol, from oxidizing and creating plaque on walls of our arteries. Plaque is what builds up over time and clogs our pipes. According to a press release from Chicago's Field Museum, "Contrary to the popular misconception, eating of chocolate does not raise blood cholesterol levels. Chocolate contains stearic acid, which is a neutral fat that doesn't raise bad cholesterol (LDL).

"Also, the cocoa butter in chocolate contains oleic acid, a good monounsaturated fat similar to that fat found in olive oil that may actually raise good cholesterol."

The celestially divine chocolate contains an intriguing substance called theobromine, a stimulant that is chemically similar to caffeine. Theobromine, meaning "food of the gods," is a substance found in cacao. Because it dilates the arteries, it is used to treat high blood pressure.

Cocoa also contains phenylethylamine, or PEA, a compound that increases your production of adrenaline and dopamine, which are mood elevators. PEA is also the same chemical our Earth Suits produce when we are happy or in love. Pass the chocolates—I'm feeling better all ready!

And if that wasn't enough, a 1996 study cited by *Nature* magazine reported that chocolate contains small amounts of anandamine, a substance that is similar to the mood-altering chemicals in marijuana. *Peace, love, and five in a tub!*

But not all chocolates are created equally. Various processing procedures of cheaper brands can deplete chocolate of the beneficial nutrients, and their levels may vary from brand to brand. High-quality dark chocolate is the best, and chocolate made with

cocoa butter rather than the cheaper palm oils is much better for your heart. Read the ingredients and nutrition information labels carefully.

Most studies do not address how much chocolate in needed to achieve heart-healthy benefits, nor do they mention any long-term benefits or risks of eating chocolate. But don't think that more is better. Some sources state that you shouldn't consume more than one ounce per day of dark, semi-sweet chocolate in a cocoa butter base. Is that clear? Forrest Gump said, "Life is like a box of chocolates." You just can't eat the whole box at once.

Consider that when something sounds too good to be true, it usually is. Chocolate can have a dark side. For example, there are some claims that it triggers allergies, the jitters, migraines, and occasionally, upset tummies. There is, however, little evidence to support these claims.

So, don't stop enjoying chocolate. Eat it, but in moderation, since we know that consuming fruits, vegetables, green tea and red wine are far better choices for lowering cholesterol. How about chocolate-dipped fruit?

Who eats the most chocolate? Well, it's not in Africa, where most of our chocolate is grown, nor in Asia. About 1.1 million tons were produced in the Ivory Coast. The country's government estimates that the livelihood of half the country's fourteen million people is directly or indirectly tied to cacao production. The Chinese, for example, eat only one bar of chocolate for every thousand eaten by the British.

Mexicans use chocolate more as a drink and a spice than as a candy. You might eat more chocolate in one of their famous mole sauces.

One might guess that Americans eat the most chocolate coming in at an average of twelve pounds per person per year. According the Field Museum, in 1998, that came to 3.3 billion pounds. Americans spend around 13 billion per year on the food of the gods. Are you doing your part?

But the Europeans definitely are the largest consumers. As far back as the late 1700s, the people of Madrid, Spain consumed nearly 12 million pounds of chocolate a year. Today, fifteen of the sixteen leading per-capita chocolate-consuming countries are in Europe, with the Swiss leading the charge. As of 1998, the United States was ninth, but we can try harder.

Please listen to me closely: Any of my friends or beloved family members who may be planning to send me a hollow Easter bunny this year should forget it. Solid only, please.

> *'Twill make Old Women Young and Fresh,*
> *Create New Motions of the Flesh.*
> *And cause them long for you know what,*
> *If they but taste of chocolate.*

> James Wadsworth (1768–1844)
> *A History of the Nature and Quality of Chocolate*

Chocolate Lover's Logic

- Beans are vegetables. Therefore, chocolate is a vegetable derived from cocoa beans.
- Sugar is derived from sugar cane or sugar beets, both plants, which places it into the vegetable category. Therefore, candy bars are health food.
- Chocolate-covered raisins are my weakness. Since strawberries, orange slices, cherries, and raisins are fruit, you can eat all you want.
- Chocolate candy bars contain dairy, so they must be healthy.
- Do you know how to get two pounds of chocolate home from the grocery in a hot car? Eat it all while you're still in the parking lot.
- A balanced diet consists of one chocolate-fudge brownie with chocolate buttercream icing—in each hand.
- Another balanced diet: Savor equal parts of white chocolate and dark chocolate.
- If it were not for chocolate, there wouldn't be any need for control-top pantyhose.
- Eat chocolate. You wouldn't want to damage an entire garment industry.
- "I think I'll move to either Hershey, Pennsylvania; Cocoa Beach, Florida; or Carmel, California."
- Chocolates are full of preservatives. You'll live longer.

&

Chocolate Morsels

- More than a billion chocolate bars are made each year at the Hershey factory.
- White chocolate contains lots of cocoa butter, which

comes from cocoa beans, but it does not have the secret ingredient of all "true" chocolates: chocolate liqueur.

* M & M candies were named after their inventors: Forrest Mars and Bruce Murrie.

* As far as scientist can tell, pure chocolate does not cause pimples. And chocolate may protect your teeth against cavities. It is the sugar and other ingredients added to chocolate candy that cause problems.

* It takes almost one quart of milk to make a one-pound bar of milk chocolate.

* Many people believe the chocolate kiss was named by Mr. Hershey when his wife kissed him after she tasted his new candy. Others argue that "kiss" is an old name for any small piece of chocolate wrapped in foil.

* The first chocolate bunny was made at Disney World.

* The world's largest chocolate egg was 17 feet 9 inches tall and weighed over two and a half tons.

* Chocolate contributes less than 2 percent of the fat in the American diet. The main sources of dietary fat come from meat, full-fat dairy products, and fried foods.

* Chocolate contains very little caffeine.

* Chocolate contains copper, iron, zinc, and magnesium.

* Chocolate contains antioxidants called polyphenols, which are the same found in tea and red wine.

* People do not become addicted to chocolate. Instead, studies report, people desire chocolate because they enjoy the sensation of eating it. The mouth feel.

* More chemicals are sprayed on cocoa beans than on any other crop.

* Want organic chocolate? Go online to www.greenandblacks.com

Diabetes

A Pandemic of Modern Society

A plague! What plague?

It all innocently begins as Joe Average reverses his ball cap, mindlessly cruises up to one of the prolific fast-food drive-thru windows, and blurts, "Gimme a triple cheeseburger, extra mayo, fries—super-size those, will ya—and a large strawberry shake."

"Would you like lettuce and tomato on that, sir?" the pubescent voice inquires.

"Why, hell no, sonny, whaddya think I am, a Nancy boy? And don't be chincy with the salt!" Definitely a white bread mentality.

Sound familiar? Are you overfed, overweight, and underactive? It's an unflattering, albeit common, description of many, but not all, adults who develop diabetes in their middle years. The National Center for Chronic Disease Prevention and Health Promotion declares 17 million people—6.2 percent of the population—have diabetes, and 20 percent of all people over the age of sixty-five are diabetic.

Let's see the hands: How many of you does that include? Holy cow! Does it possibly have anything to do with the paradox that fad-obsessed Americans, desperate for their own identity, ironically follow the junk food in-crowd? "I need to have diabetes to be like everyone else." Keeping up with the Joneses turns tragically hip on the treadmill of conformity. Diabetes, the silent killer, comes with a steep price tag, rendering us vulnerable to heart disease, high blood pressure, blindness, kidney disease, nervous system disease, amputations, dental disease, and other imbalances. Charming.

WHAT IS DIABETES MELLITUS?

Diabetes mellitus, which is gaining epidemic proportions in our increasingly slothful Western civilization, is a disorder in which the body is unable to control the amount of glucose, or sugar, in the blood because the mechanism that converts sugar to energy is no longer functioning properly. In Type 1 diabetes, the pancreas doesn't produce insulin, which metabolizes glucose, and one must take insulin injections. People with Type 2 diabetes, also known as "adult onset diabetes," often can control the condition with diet, exercise, and medications.

Ascending the proverbial mountaintop seeking truth, I sought enlightenment from a fellow "gym rat," Dave Henry, a retired clinical pharmacologist/clinical endocrinologist. In between ab crunches, he shared this frank and startling information: With diabetes, the diet controls the body, even poisons it. The ingestion of glucose, the final denominator of carbohydrate metabolism, accumulates in the blood and becomes toxic. Additionally, the high levels of glucose suck water and electrolytes into the urine, leading to severe dehydration. Ketone bodies accumulate and can lead to acidosis and sometimes death. Even with appropriate insulin (or insulin-like) therapy, a major cornerstone of the treatment of diabetes is dietary control.

My solution: nutritional consciousness paired with educated consumption.

WHAT IS THE GLYCEMIC INDEX?

No longer referred to as "sugar diabetes," glucose diabetes is more like it. For my feeble layman's mind, Dave dumbed down the glycemic index (GI): Simply stated, the glycemic index relates the

increase in blood glucose concentration produced for each gram of glucose ingested for each specific food. The index is highest for glucose itself and lower for complex carbohydrates like unrefined whole grains.

Something as simple as choosing natural unrefined whole grains, the way our Creator intended, instead of processed, helps protect our loving families from diabetes and a multitude of degenerative diseases. The National Institutes of Health claims there are no known methods to prevent Type 1, or juvenile, diabetes. The concentration of glucose, the final denominator of carbohydrate metabolism, accumulates in the blood and is toxic.

On the bright side, several clinical trials are currently in progress searching for a cure. The assumption: Too much glucose in any form is toxic. Please don't deceive yourself. One can OD on sugar. The "white stuff" can kill you just as surely as cocaine and heroin. *Zoom, crash, and burn!*

White often represents purity, simplicity, and perfection. However, white foods with high glycemic indices are *unnecessary* and should be avoided. These white villains include processed sugar, hulled white rice, baking potatoes, all-purpose bleached flour, white bread, white flour pasta, conventional cow's milk, marshmallows, whipped cream, non-dairy whipped toppings, mayonnaise, flavored artificial coffee creamers, and, sadly, white chocolate.

WHITE BREAD: THE STAFF OF LIFE?

Historically, big industry hasn't done society many healthy favors. For example, will someone please explain the logic of Wonder Bread returning the eleven vitamins and minerals back into the bread? Where'd they go? Did Uncle Ben really do us a favor by hulling his famous rice? When steely-cold industrial machinery crushes whole grains into lifeless white flour, their delicate vitality is destroyed. So when you make grilled cheese on white bread for

your family, they, too, become devitalized. Garbage in, garbage out. Soft and wimpy white bread, the scourge of the new millennium.

When vitamin-packed whole wheat is pulverized into all-purpose white flour, it loses 80 percent of its nutrients. But there's more: When it's heated in the oven, the nutrients change chemically, destroying some and altering others into nonusable ones. Offer your family delicious whole grains breads and other unprocessed complex carbohydrates.

COLON POW! THE FIBER FACTOR.

Fiber speed-bumps glucose as it travels through your bloodstream, therefore reducing peaks and valleys of blood sugar levels. The American Dietetic Association recommends twenty to thirty-five grams of fiber per day, but most Americans ingest only a measly twelve grams daily.

LOOK OUT!

If you've avoided fiber so far in life, I must warn you! Begin adding fiber to your diet gradually, just a few grams a day, until your delicate Earth Suit adjusts to the additional, colon-cleansing substance. The bathroom event should take moments, not fifteen painful and hemorrhoid-producing minutes.

Too much fiber too soon will render you rumbling, bloaty, and gassy, and result in a lovely bout with diarrhea. Be gradual. Furthermore, when eating a fibrous diet, water is absolutely essential to keep the pipes running smoothly. Researchers at the University of Minnesota report families that regularly include whole grains in their diet have a lower risk of diabetes, irritable bowel syndrome and other gastric maladies.

To early Native Americans, diabetes was unknown. Today, they have the highest incidence in the country. *How?* It's a sad story. When forced away from their sacred land and natural way of eating, they were placed into reservations where their only menu was the "white man's diet" of overly refined foods with a high GI. American Indians didn't eat refined corn, processed sugar, or devitalized grains. They knew better. We, however, should have no "reservations" about learning from our native brothers and sisters.

Regular aerobic exercise is also a must and shouldn't be downplayed. Obesity is an overwhelming risk factor for developing diabetes. My friend Dave reminds me too that caloric excess—pigging out—is by far the most important factor (other than genetics) in the etiology of Type 2 diabetes. Science continually proves that less is more, but powerful, influential TV and print media advertisers keep pounding the message that more is better down the throats of our children and grandchildren. Perhaps the medium truly is the message.

Our friends at the American Diabetes Association report that a 1997 study showed the annual total direct and indirect cost of diabetes to be a wallet-flattening $98 billion. Big bucks—$2.5 billion—also go to the makers of Metformin, a drug that fights diabetes. Sadly, it appears that this disease is rather profitable.

Facetiously speaking, the only way science can solve this plague is by declaring diabetes nonexistent throughout the United States. That way, all the endocrinologists have to say is that any patient insisting that they have diabetes will be rediagnosed as being paranoid, and hence ineligible for medical care, as mental health benefits are essentially nonexistent in most managed care plans. Problem solved.

Yes, eating healthy in today's society requires strong individual effort. Conformity blows. Be eccentric. Practice homefront, nutritional stewardship. *Your body's your buddy.*

Cheese

DON'T LET THE CURDS GET IN THE WHEY

I'm a Cheese Whiz man,
I like to suck it from a can.

Anonymous

It was, I believe, vegetarian Grace Slick—the Martha Stewart of Rock—who recently gave cheese the label of "liquid meat."

When I became a vegetarian, I did a lot of soul-searching, especially when it came to cheese. But then, when I recollected Ms. Slick did more than her share of hallucinogens in the 1960s, I rationalized that it was cool to eat the right sort of cheese since, as far as I know, no critters are killed in the process. Besides, cheese has a number of unique health attributes and can be part of your family's healthy diet. Personally, I view cheese as a cooperative gift from our little animal buddies.

Growing up in Indiana didn't afford me the opportunity to sample the multitudes of marvelous cheeses in the world. Velveeta, pimento spread, American, and Parmesan from a can were all that existed in our narrow cheese view of the world. And what was it, and still is, with aerosol cheese—oh my! Cheese in a can is what paint-by-numbers is to great art. Once, after a night of generously liquid-influenced youthful partying, I blindly stumbled into the bathroom where I proceeded to brush my teeth with spray Cheez Whiz. Could have been worse.

My grandchildren now tell me there's a new cheese. "Grandpa, ever hear of *frumunda* cheese?"

"Nope," I answer.

"You know, Grandpa—it's that cheese that smells like it came 'from unda' something." They giggle and run away clutching their noses.

Americans are in love with cheese, and everyone has a favorite. Whether it be soft, semi-soft, firm, hard, or a specialty cheese, hungry fromage devotees suck, tuck, melt, cut, fold, mold, smack, pack, and eat cheese on just about every imaginable food. But please, don't squirt it!

If you thought you had to avoid cheese in the name of healthy eating, well, the times, they are a-changin'. Cheese is no longer a forbidden food. Yes, many cheeses are high in fat and calories, but they are a good source of calcium, says nutritionist Gayle Reichler, author of *Active Wellness*. Plus, cheese contains conjugated linoleic acid, the "good" fat that helps reduce the risk of cancer, heart disease, and diabetes. Cheese also contains important nutrients like protein, riboflavin, and phosphorous.

For many diners, however, all that matters is the extreme volume of molten, gooey, cheese pooling atop the deep-dish pizza or their super-sized cow burger with double bacon. For others, the "gift of the animal" is as esoteric as wine. Both creations are richly steeped in tradition, art, science, history, survival, passion, and cultural pride. Where would wine and beer be without cheese, I ask?

I have had the pleasure of grilling one of the big cheeses of the world-famous, award-winning Cabot Creamery Cooperative, nestled in the White Mountains near hospitable Montpelier, Vermont.

The Cabot Cooperative has been in continuous operation since 1919, when ninety-four farmers founded it for five dollars per cow plus a cord of wood each. Not much has changed for the farm families who own Cabot today. Up each day before the rooster's crow to milk the willing herds, and in the barns after dusk to put

the girls to bed, Cabot's farmers remain committed to preserving their way of life and to producing the finest, most flavorful cheddar on the planet.

Highly regarded *Cook's Illustrated* magazine recommends Cabot Sharp Vermont Cheddar Cheese. "This cheese came in first place in both the grilled cheese and the raw cheese tastings. Tasters liked its approachable flavor, described as 'sharp,' 'clean,' and 'tangy.' In a grilled cheese sandwich, it was 'buttery' and 'mellow' without being even the slightest bit greasy."

What Cabot brings into the barn is a clean environment. Vermont milk is considered to be among the finest and freshest in the world. Pure, fresh, wholesome milk from happy cows, excellent quality control, and an adherence to traditional cheese-making methods all add up to three Blue Ribbons at the American Cheese Society's Eighteenth Annual Conference. The ACS has honored Cabot with a "Best Cheddar" award four times in the last decade. I personally think American cheeses are superior to the European varieties. No wonder the French are so cheesed.

The cheese gospel, according to Cabot, shares the legend that coloring was originally added to cheese in order to distinguish where particular cheddars were made, thus yellow cheeses derive their color from additives. Cabot's cheddars, as well as many others made in the New England states, do not use color additives, thereby retaining the cheeses' natural white color we've not grown accustomed to. White has always represented purity, and anyone who knows me will attest that I am a staunch advocate of eating clean, unprocessed, preservative and coloring-free foods made with all-natural ingredients. Thank you, Cabot!

Fretting about the fat? Take note: *Diabetes Forecast* magazine endorsed and rated Cabot Vermont Cheddar Cheese by saying: "This reduced fat cheese is about the best we've seen. Good, real flavor, without a rubbery texture, and it melts! The fat is reduced to 4.5 grams per one ounce serving as compared with 9 grams of fat in full-fatted cheese. This cheese has about seventy calories per ounce. The Vermont Cheddar was the best."

Family Circle magazine commented: "Cabot 50 percent light cheddar and jalapeño cheddar have great hints of classic cheddar sharpness. Try for a guilt-free, grilled cheese sandwich." Do you need any more encouragement?

But what about our lactose-intolerant friends? Recent research in the *New England Journal of Medicine* study, conducted by renowned gastroenterologists, found tens of thousands of Americans might be mistakenly diagnosing themselves as lactose-intolerant. Berta McDonald, Cabot's senior vice president of marketing, quotes the author of the study. "Hard cheeses are so low in lactose that people could consume almost unlimited quantities without bringing on any lactose intolerance-related symptoms." For more information, you can call Cabot Creamery at 1-888-792-2268 or visit them on the Web at www.cabotcheese.com.

WARNING: NOT ALL CHEESES ARE CREATED EQUAL

Pasteurized cheeses, which are marked so on their labels, are safe and also an excellent source of protein and calcium. However, cheeses made from unpasteurized milk may contain harmful bacteria such as listeria, which may cause problems ranging from something as merely inconvenient as a case of the trots, to things as serious as miscarriage or premature labor. If you eat soft cheeses such as feta and brie, always make sure that they are from pasteurized milks. In general, cream cheese and cottage cheese are safe, as are hard, pasteurized cheeses such as cheddar.

POOR COWS

Soulless commercial cheeses are made by bleaching the product

(thus destroying their oil soluble vitamins), after which dyes, sorbic acid (a mold inhibitor), and synthetic vitamins are usually added. This is on top of the toxic chemicals found in the milk itself, such as pesticides, herbicides, bovine growth hormones, pus, synthetic vitamins, and penicillin. Synthetic vitamins remove minerals and calcium salts from our Earth Suits, and there are additional chemicals used in cattle forage. That's *not* the way God planned it!

The state of Vermont has some outstanding standards set in place for its dairy industry. At times, I kind of wish I could be a Vermont dairy cow, ala Woody Jackson. What a life: good hours, scenic views, warm hands on a cold New England morning, environmentally compassionate handlers, clean air and water, free grazing, room and board, all embraced by a generous wedge of good karma.

FOOD OF THE ANCIENTS

Archaeologists have discovered that as far back as 6000 B.C., cheese was made from cows' and goats' milk and stored in jars. A popular legend has it that cheese was first made in the Middle East by an unknown nomad who is said to have filled an animal-stomach saddlebag with milk to sustain him on a journey, by horse, across the desert. After several hours he stopped to quench his thirst, only to discover the milk had separated into a pale watery liquid and solid white lumps. The combination of the milk's coagulating enzyme known as rennin, the hot sun, and the movement of the horse effectively caused the milk to separate into curds and whey. The nomad found the whey drinkable and the curds palatable. The moral: Never let curds get in the whey of a good thing.

The cheese gods inform us that cheese should always be refrigerated, between thirty-five to forty degrees Fahrenheit, and in its original wrapping until use. Once cheese is exposed to air, mold and dehydration may occur. Protect your cheese and always work with it in a clean area, and keep it in a clean, airtight wrapping.

As it is with any animal-derived food, for optimum health and enjoyment of cheese, practice variety, balance, and moderation. Lobbing several pounds of cheese onto your two slices of pizza is an abuse of your relationship with it.

As a final word, cheesaphobes, loosen up! Let us celebrate the beauty and natural symbiosis between humans and animals. Go hug a cow and shake the milking hand of all hard-working farmers for all the good cheese they produce—a true human's and animal's co-op! Our relationship with the all of creation is vital to the survival of both.

Probiotics

OUR FIRST LINE OF DEFENSE
IN THE WARRING GARDEN OF EATIN'

Would anyone join me for a chilled, full-bodied, fruity mouthful of microbial bacteria?

Whether you find the concept palatable or not, bacteria are our friends. Like the Skipper of the SS *Minnow*, we'd be lost without our little microbial buddies. You may find this hard to digest, but we are, in essence, a walking ecosystem, home to trillions of microorganisms. Your gums, teeth, hair, and skin teem with countless varieties of . . . gasp, yes . . . bacterial microbes.

More microorganisms—an estimated one hundred different species—live inside your gastrointestinal tract. That's more than there are people in the world, or have been in all of history. Think about that the next time you're feeling lonely.

Individuals with a healthy balance of intestinal colonies of these symbiotic warriors are equipped to fend off invasions and subsequent occupations of harmful pathogens that can cause everything from infections of the mouth, urinary tract infections, and a whole host of lower GI afflictions ranging from chronic flatulence to constipation and diarrhea.

As we age, our Earth Suits contain fewer beneficial microbes and need a little help from their friends. Not possessing the proper balance of microflora can lead to digestion hassles, thwart absorption of valuable vitamins and nutrients, and foster an increased

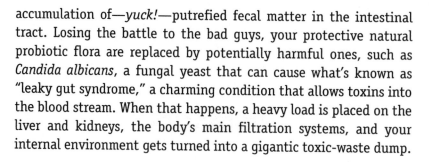

accumulation of—*yuck!*—putrefied fecal matter in the intestinal tract. Losing the battle to the bad guys, your protective natural probiotic flora are replaced by potentially harmful ones, such as *Candida albicans*, a fungal yeast that can cause what's known as "leaky gut syndrome," a charming condition that allows toxins into the blood stream. When that happens, a heavy load is placed on the liver and kidneys, the body's main filtration systems, and your internal environment gets turned into a gigantic toxic-waste dump.

DIGESTION: DON'T HESITATE, LET'S MASTICATE

Remember the old days when your mom told you not to gulp down your food and to chew it carefully? Nowadays it seems that most Americans wolf their food down as if someone's going to take it away from them. As if it isn't bad enough that the portions are super-sized, they're frequently only half-chewed, all in the name of "gotta hurry."

Your Earth Suit's successful absorption of food's glorious nutrition begins in the mouth. That's where mastication takes place and chemical digestion begins. Furthermore, the chewing process stimulates the production of digestive enzymes in the stomach and small intestine, which is where the breakdown of carbohydrates and fats takes place.

It's in the twenty-one or so feet of small intestine that the army of microorganisms really gets to work. Under ideal circumstances, detent exists in your Earth Suit's internal flora garden, but now and then bad microbes try to take dominance. The skirmish begins when "evil" bacteria infiltrate. The staunch defenders of our health, probiotic microflora, are thrown out of nature's normal balance, which can result in something as minor as a tummy ache to major health consequences, including loss of stamina and energy, and a weakened immune system.

Here's a constipating thought: Our gastrointestinal tracts are attacked daily by hordes of harmful bacterial invaders, and our resistance is diminished by "conveniences" of modern living— overzealous use of antibiotics, antibacterial products (such as hand soaps), radiation, antacids, junk food, alcohol, chlorine, prescription medications, and diets high in saturated fat and sugar. Pesticide and herbicide residue on fresh produce can also whack out your good flora, so always wash produce thoroughly as if your family's lives depended on it.

CAN'T WE ALL JUST GET ALONG?

Have no fear, the cure is here in the form of probiotics. The opposite of antibiotics, probiotic organisms are the peacemakers for our GI tracts. These "good guys" help balance intestinal microflora and keep down the growth of bad bacterial terrorists. This tricky maneuvering encourages healthy digestion and absorption of nutrients, as well as promoting immune function and thus increasing the body's resistance to infection.

According to the *Colon Health Handbook,* a healthy colon should contain at least 85 percent lactobacillus and 15 percent coliform bacteria. However, the typical colon has just the opposite bacterial balance, which results in a plethora of digestive upsets such as excessive gassiness, bloating, and constipation, as well as malabsorption of nutrients, which can lead to an overgrowth of candida.

Lactobacillus acidophilus and *Lactobacillus bifidus* are the two main probiotic species setting up house in our GI tracts. *L. acidophilus,* found in yogurt and kefir, is essential for the absorption of nutrients. It also activates production of vitamins B12 and K and aids in lactose tolerance and digestion.

L. acidophilus has an antibacterial effect that helps detoxify harmful substances in our systems. Antibiotics, oral contraceptives, aspirin, corticosteroids, poor diet, and stress can cause an

imbalance of the "friendly bacteria." The good flora found in acidophilus bind with some of the unfriendly substances, causing them to be excreted.

L. bifidus is the predominant organism in the intestinal flora and establishes a healthy environment for the manufacture of the B-complex vitamins and vitamin K. For women, *L. bifidus* help fight vaginal yeast infections by destroying the pathogenic organisms causing the problem.

L. bifidus also helps keep intestines healthy by aiding peristalsis—the muscular "wave" that moves things along—resulting in softer, smoother stools and destroying and eliminating harmful bacteria and waste toxins that accumulate in the intestines.

It's exciting to note that probiotic organisms, which have been studied for fifty years, are now mentioned in the same sentence as cancer prevention. In vitro experiments have indicated that the probiotics in some dairy products can reduce the impact of some known carcinogenic mutagens and inhibit the growth of cancer cells. We've all heard of sturdy Siberians who eat yogurt all their lives and live to well past the age of one hundred, although genetics and vodka probably play a significant role. Even so, my redheaded nephews in New England were raised on yogurt, and they grew quite tall, vibrantly healthy, and quite intelligent. Good genes? Perhaps.

Now, if someone could make just beer-flavored yogurt, we could really rock the world.

READ THE LABELS

Studies conclude the highest quality probiotic supplements contain live cultures and starter nutrients so the probiotics can be fed and grow strong enough to establish a healthy army of friendly bacteria.

Yogurt and kefir (my favorite) are the most obvious probiotic

food sources. However, to be really effective, about 4 million to 10 million viable culture organisms are needed, and one container of yogurt does not contain nearly enough of the beneficial microbes, nor the variety needed to fight the battle.

Make good quantities of yogurt and kefir a part of your daily diet, and to ensure you get the probiotics you need, look for the words "live active cultures" on the ingredient labels. Some products go into more detail on their labeling, however, so when you check the labels, besides the ones I've already mentioned, here are some other micro-buddies to look for:

- *Lactobacillus bulgaricus* does the same job as *L. acidophilus*.
- *Streptococcus thermophilus* inhibits harmful bacteria, enhances digestion of milk, and some strains produce antibiotic substances.
- *Lactobacillus rhamnosus* is a relatively new kid on the probiotic block, and helps prevent infections, including fungal and bacterial vaginal infections.

In the end, what it's all about is maintaining a healthy balance inside our bodies, our minds, our spirits, and in our hectic lives. We spend absurd amounts of time, money, and effort keeping the exterior of our Earth Suits clean, well groomed, and attractive. It's just as important, if not more so, to maintain a healthy, internal, digestive environment. Our digestive systems are somewhat like tree roots. When the roots are healthy, the tree is strong. But if the roots have problems, the whole tree suffers.

Outward beauty comes from being healthy inside. When you're insides are healthy, it's reflected in your glowing energy, good skin color and tone, and sparkling hair and eyes. So, fight the good probiotic fight, and those spunky microbes just might be your ticket to a long, disease-free furlough.

Quinoa

THE MOTHER GRAIN

May I introduce you to very old friend from the past? The name is quinoa (*keen-wa*), food of the future. Can it be that one little seed is all we need?

Long ago, in early America, white settlers began what I suppose could be called the first "urban sprawl." They were firm in the belief that they had to "save" the souls of and control the "savage and pagan" Indians, who ate mushrooms, communicated with their gods, revered nature, and were deeply devoted stewards of the earth and all of creations and bountiful resources set in place. The white settlers found this philosophy unfathomable and felt threatened by it. Thus, the frontier pioneers chose to dominate and exploit not only the Indians, but also the earth's resources for their own profit and personal gain. They rationalized that according to the Bible, it was cool to subdue and exploit. Among the resources they exploited was the buffalo, which they nearly succeeded in making extinct.

What's this have to do with quinoa, you ask?

Historians indicate the same cultural arrogance that was seen in North America occurred in South America when the Spaniard Conquistadors invaded. For eight thousand years, people living high in the Andes in the Lake Titicaca area of Bolivia began to cultivate quinoa. Quinoa was a key factor in the rise of the Incan empire, allowing the people to be self-sufficient. The Incas drank chicha, a

beer made from fermented quinoa and celebrated it by offering sacrifices of animals, children, food, and cloth. *Children?*

In 1532, Francisco Pizarro, a Spanish explorer, reached the Andes with a small army of 158 men, and within a year they destroyed the quinoa fields, killed the Inca god-king, and forced the Inca culture into submission. *Freakin' bullies!* Much like the American Indian and the buffalo, the daily lives of the Incas had revolved around the growing, harvesting, eating and honoring of quinoa. Eager to bring the Incas under their control, Pizarro not only forbade the ceremonial rituals that centered on quinoa, but even outlawed the planting of the grain. Wipe out a culture's main food source and you can wipe out the culture. The rationale is that the quickest way to destroy a civilization is to desecrate what they consider to be sacred. Cases of malnutrition escalated along with a high infant mortality rate.

In her book *The Splendid Grain*, Rebecca Wood tells us that by the 1800s, the "Mother Grain" was almost totally suppressed by the Spanish. Good news: Quinoa is now on a comeback and is being considered for food programs in South American countries because of its magnificent nutritional value. When Wood asked a Calaway Indian herbalist about the folklore swirling around the medicinal properties of quinoa, he gave her a special variety of quinoa that he scooped with a tiny seashell. Then he told her, "Quinoa is medicine for soul calling. When a person's soul is out or has sunk into the ground, give him a massage with quinoa and then bury the grain on the spot where the problem first manifested."

Quinoa today

In 1982, David F. Schnorr, president of the Quinoa Corporation, brought the first fifty-pound bag of this hitherto unknown grain into the U.S. to introduce it to the natural foods industry. America greatly thanks you, Mr. Schnorr.

Dave shares with us that quinoa (*Chenopodium quinoa*) is a member of the goosefoot family, which includes beets, chard, and spinach. Quinoa's appearance is similar to millet but with grains that are a bit smaller and whiter.

Mother Nature created this tiny, quite potent grain. Check this out: Quinoa possesses large quantities of calcium, "good" fat, iron, and phosphorus, and B vitamins, more so than many other grains. Just two ounces of quinoa offers 14 percent of the RDA for B6. Niacin, one of the important B vitamins, totals an impressive 2.49 mg. Pretty convincing. One-half cup uncooked quinoa contains 51 mg of lean, clean, complete plant protein, an impressive 629 mg potassium, 2.8 mg zinc, 42 mcg folic acid, 7.9 mg iron, and 179 mg magnesium. There's also 5 grams of colon-cleansing fiber in that same half cup, which is 50 percent higher than wheat.

This light and easy-to-digest "mother grain" contains ten amino acids, including lysine, which may be capable of loosening and preventing nasty deposits, keeping our artery walls clean and flexible. Naturally, this would lessen one's susceptibility for high blood pressure, a major factor in heart attack and stroke. Lysine also insures the adequate absorption of calcium, helps form collagen (which makes up bone cartilage and connective tissues), and aids in the production of antibodies, hormones, and enzymes. Recent studies have shown that lysine may be effective against herpes by improving the balance of nutrients that reduce viral growth. A lysine deficiency may contribute to tiredness, inability to concentrate, irritability, bloodshot eyes, retarded growth, hair loss, anemia, and reproductive problems. *Oh, Lord, pass the quinoa now!*

To sum it up, this remarkably nutritious "super grain" can supply us with all of our Earth Suit's requirements: complex carbohydrates, fats, amino acids, complete protein, vitamins, minerals, and fiber. Quinoa is also gluten-free, perfect for those with allergies. Can a cow-burger and deep fried cheese-fries from the Porcelain Palace compare?

The Incas advised using ground and cooked quinoa as a poultice to draw out pain and discoloration from bruises. It was used as a

diuretic and to encourage vomiting. The Indians included quinoa in their treatment of urinary tract infections, tuberculosis, appendicitis, liver problems, altitude sickness, and motion sickness. Because of its high calcium content, it's considered beneficial in treating bone problems. And due to its high protein and complex carbohydrate composition, the Andean people even now consider it an endurance food and include it as a daily staple. Sounds like something the bone-crunching, bruising National Basketball Association might want to give to its players.

Cooking techniques and tips

Quinoa has a saponin coating, which is its protection from birds and the intense rays of the altiplano sun. Therefore, before cooking, you must rinse, rinse, and then rinse again to remove the saponin. Otherwise, the grain will taste quite bitter and could actually be somewhat toxic. Got that? Just use a fine mesh strainer and rinse for two full minutes.

Quinoa is milder than brown rice and will not dominate or suck the flavor from a dish. I personally love the plain, nutty grain by itself, but a light dry roasting or sautéing before cooking will bring fuller flavor. (This works with any grain.) The quinoa will absorb flavors from whatever oils, herbs, and/or spices used in cooking. Cooking proportions are one part quinoa to two parts water. To avoid burning the delicate grains, bring the water to a boil, add the quinoa, reduce heat, cover the pot, and simmer. The quick-cooking grain will be ready in about ten to fifteen minutes. Then you can proudly serve it, replacing the usual starchy, nutritionally bankrupt white rice or potatoes. Some chefs blushingly admit quinoa resembles a flagellating sperm when properly cooked.

I predict that within this twenty-first century, a much wiser society will look back and recognize the fast-food industry for what it really is: greedy, soulless, highly efficient purveyors of illness and premature death. Sad but true, our children and grandchildren will suffer the most since television has more influence on them than their parents.

If history does indeed repeat itself, we'd better quickly learn from it. Remember—the quickest way to destroy a civilization is to destroy what is considered sacred.

You can deploy quinoa to the frontlines of nutritional defense and fortify the bodies, minds, and souls of those you love.

If you'd like to learn more about Ancient Harvest Quinoa, check out Quinoa Corporation's Web site www.quinoa.net, e-mail them at quinoacorp@aol.com, or write to the address below. They'll be delighted to answer your questions about ancient grains.

Quinoa Corporation
P.O. Box 279
Gardena, California 90248

"Live" Food

THE TASTE OF LIFE

The next time someone tells you to eat it raw, kindly reply, "Okey-dokey!"

In today's "vege-phobic" pop culture, you might consider that the unconventional foods seen on NBC's popular *Fear Factor* might be used in another fashion. What if, for $50,000, TV-land substituted raw produce in lieu of tasty, putrefied Limburger cheese covered with squirming maggots? I'd venture the young competitors would probably drop like, well, flies in a bug zapper.

It seems that, regardless of age, people turn up their noses at plant foods and consider them, as my granddaughter Morgan says, "Yucky."

I used to be among them. Growing up in the Midwest, the thought of eating anything raw made my stomach turn. Our home life centered around Mom's kitchen, where she produced gorgeous, flaky-crusted pies, succulent beef roasts, smoky ham-flavored green beans, and soft, white, buttery yeast rolls. Boomers also developed the tradition of tons o' dead barm animals smoking away on Weber grills, and you were considered downright pinko if you didn't eat that way.

In spite of all this, a raw foods diet seems to be on the popular

upswing. Already in America, more than thirty raw foods restaurants have opened, and the diet was featured on *Sex in the City*. I wonder, though, whether this "bioactive" food mania is the ultimate back-to-nature diet, or if it's just another fad diet du jour with influential celebrities lining up to nosh on raw broccoli and tempeh steaks. I've always maintained that fad diets were like using Band-aids to treat a sucking chest wound.

Eating raw foods for health is nothing new. The concept dates back about twenty-five hundred years, when the great mathematician and teacher Pythagoras used raw foods to heal people who suffered from poor digestion and other maladies. A few hundred years later, the Essenes, who established communities in the Middle East, were said to chow on primarily live foods and were reported by historians to live an average of a hundred and twenty years. Of course one must also factor in genetics and calorie content.

Here's the poop: The raw diet is based on our consuming only unprocessed, organic, whole-plant-based foods, of which at least 75 percent should be uncooked. The diet consists of organic fresh fruits and vegetables, nuts, tempeh, edamame, seeds, beans, grains, dried fruits, seaweeds, freshly made fruit juices, purified water, and milk from young coconuts, not lactating bovines. Raw, living foods possess essential, underestimated living food enzymes, and "rawists" gently warn us that cooking plant foods above 116 degrees destroys those enzymes. They are correct. Enzymes are a huge deal since they are considered the life force of a food. Studies show, however, that an eighty-year-old has one-thirtieth the amount of enzymes as an eighteen-year-old. Enzymes manufactured in the pancreas help us digest food completely, and contain the power of the life force itself, transforming and storing precious energy. So, one can assume that as we age, we definitely should "eat it raw."

The process of cooking foods also destroys premium, top-shelf vitamins and minerals. Furthermore, cooked foods not only take longer to digest, but they also allow partially digested fats, protein, and carbohydrates to clog up our plumbing. Even so, some folks have reservations about dining on raw, however. My gym buddy Dave Henry, a retired Eli Lilly biochemist, tells me "the first thing that strikes me about raw food is the possibility for microbial contamination—remember the problem with scallions and hepatitis? Regular soybeans cannot be eaten raw because of indigestible lectins that will give you the trots; however, after boiling or pressure-cooking these gems, these culprits are destroyed. Deliciously protein rich, nutty fermented tempeh and creamy miso are made from soymilk, a *heat* extract of soybeans." Powerful nutrients appear in noble soy foods prepared by traditional fermentation methods, such as miso, tempeh, and natto. For the highest quality, please, go to a whole foods store and buy fresh, organic versions.

The practice of eating whole, raw foods is practiced by all species on earth, except for man and our domesticated animal buddies. Our dogs and cats suffer from a variety of the same debilitating conditions as humans on diets of highly processed cooked foods, such as obesity, arthritis, heart disease, and diabetes. However, research shows that if animals were left to their own natural eating devices, this would likely not be the case. Might that define why arrogant America is number one of the developed countries in cancer, heart disease, arthritis, obesity, hypertension, MS, mortality rates, miscarriages, and birth deformities? We eat more meat, more protein, and more saturated fat than any other nation. Not a statistic to be proud of.

Our unsound Western diet speeds up aging and encourages chronic degenerative diseases at an earlier age. Our Creator, through the miracle of nature, has designed us so that our ill health can be reversed with a food-based multivitamin supplementation, and by eating more raw, balanced, plant-based meals, exercise, and with, of course, the assistance of a family doctor. Enzymes may be purchased as supplements, but fresh, organic, raw food is your best source.

My glowing rawist friends claim that live plant foods supply all that we need to be at our highest level of awareness and health. My pal Kathie Gullick says, "If you've never tried a month of your life

on a live plant food diet, you have never known how ill you were or how simply marvelous you can feel."

The raw foods diet heals, without a doubt. My only concern is that all conventional and organic farm produce have nasty pathogens left by some critter as a gift that might be lurking on the food's surface: germs and bacteria ready to give us a case of the runs, E. coli, staph, or salmonella. Casual washing might miss these things, and even cooking to 116 degrees may not kill them. Therefore, this eco-friendly diet takes diligence and dedication, much like the macrobiotic diet, but it surely beats becoming fertilizer. As Louis Pasteur said on his deathbed: "The microbe is nothing. The terrain is everything."

Let this tidbit dissolve in your mouth: According to *Fungalbionics: The Fungal/Mycotoxin Etiology of Human Disease* (vol. 2. Freiberg, Germany: Johann Friedrich Oberlin Verlag, 1994), the average American meal (meat, dairy, fish) contains 750 million to 1 billion pathogenic microorganisms, whereas the average vegan meal has a piddly 500. Don't sweat it, just wash it.

When my wife and I embraced vegetarianism, becoming fond of vegetables was indeed awkward at first. Sweet, juicy fruits were no sweat, and the variety of grains, legumes, and soy that provided complex carbohydrates were easy to adjust to. But those crunchy vegetables? That was another story.

We decided variety, education, and perseverance would help us evolve. As part of our daily dinner ritual, Sandi and I would pick a seasonal vegetable, study its history and nutritional perks, then prepare it either steamed, poached, nuked, baked, or lightly grilled as the star of the show. Eating with the seasons is part of the journey.

I've noticed that most Americans would rather gulp their food rather than chew it. With that in mind, I suggest that you include the all-purpose smoothie in your diet. It's a fun and quick way to get five to six of your required daily seven to nine portions of raw fruits and vegetables. Just toss chunks of your favorite fresh, organic, seasonal fruits, into your blender, then add just enough

orange juice or apple cider to enable the mixture to become one with the Cosmos. Want vegetables? Wash and scrub a carrot—do not peel it—then cut it into small pieces and whip that sucker into oblivion. Go one nutritional step further and add silken tofu, soy protein, whey powder, or organic yogurt, and you've got a power meal, baby. (The proteins, in this instance, are cooked.) Our grandkids call smoothies "juicilicious." A word of caution: Calories quickly add up on this type of smoothie diet, so, as with other good things, practice moderation.

The raw foods diet rocks, and it's environmentally friendly. By eating a live plant food diet, we free up our metabolic process so that our Earth Suits can heal, restore, and rejuvenate the body, mind, and spirit. Healthy, delicious vegetarian cuisine made with living foods can magically reverse lingering health problems. At home, make it a ritual to wash and scrub your plant foods as if your loving family's lives depended on it.

My advice: Just shut up and eat it raw! You have everything to gain healthwise and nothing to lose but unwanted pounds.

I recommend these good raw foods cookbooks:
> *The Complete Book of Raw Food*, Lori Bard, ed.
>   (Hatherleigh Press)

> *Rainbow Green Live-Food Cuisine* by Gabriel Cousens, M.D.
>   (North Atlantic Books and Essene Vision Books)

Honey

The Other Vitamin Bee?

The Owl and the Pussycat went to sea
In a beautiful pea-green boat,
They took some honey, and plenty of money,
Wrapped up in a five-pound note.

Edward Lear (1812–1888)

Spending relaxed, sunset moments in my garden is pure bliss. The hours spent tilling the raw earth render me transfixed in wonder and awe of nature's myriad of esoteric activities, mesmerized by dutiful insects, busily, doing "what comes naturally."

When I was a mere redheaded curly-top child, honey was a rare treat served on feathery-soft white bread, slathered with creamy butter. The only other thing I knew about honey was what the TV Westerns taught me: Honey spread on a white man's body by "savage" Indians was quite an efficient way to attract fire ants.

But there's so much more! Of all the garden insects, bees are probably the most curious, organized, and socialized group—and likely the most productive. As you stir an amber teaspoon of honey into your steaming chamomile tea, sip on this: The average honeybee makes one-twelfth teaspoon of the delicious nectar in its very busy lifetime. Two million flowers need to be tapped, and fifty-five thousand miles must be logged to produce just one pound of honey. A bee will visit fifty to one hundred flowers during one collection

trip. Bees manufacture honey to serve as the food source for the hive during the long months of winter when flowers aren't blooming and nectar isn't available. For at least the past nine thousand years, humans have been collecting honey from honeybees. Your tea just became a ceremony, a celebration of Earth's natural, abundant bounty and mystery in symbiosis.

More than 150 million years ago, when man was nothing more than a glimmer in God's eye, bees were busy producing the world's oldest sweetener. Solitary bees appeared 25 million years ago and they became social insects about 10 million to 20 million years ago.

Archeological findings indicate that humans harvested honey from hives in rocky cliffs or hollow trees, and prehistoric cave paintings show honey harvesting.

Later on, trees holding swarms were cut down and brought close to homes where the bees could be looked after, making the honey easier to acquire, which was the beginning of beekeeping. Forty-five hundred years ago, Egyptians kept bees in artificial shelters. Pharaoh Tuthmosis III made the bee the symbol of Lower Egypt. Honey has been found in the tombs of ancient Egyptian pharaohs—and it's still edible. Because it's acidic and therefore not conducive to bacterial growth, honey never goes bad.

Furthermore, the ancient Egyptians were hip not only to honey's sweetness but also its medicinal benefits and used it to treat a variety of ailments such as cataracts, cuts, and burns. The ancient Chinese completely covered smallpox sufferers with honey to speed healing and prevent scarring.

In Greek and Roman mythology, honey was known as "ambrosia," food of the gods. Romans used honey instead of gold to pay their taxes. *Hmmm. Could that be where the phrase "sweeten the pot" originated?*

Classic Greek text from Homer, Plato, Aristotle, Democritus, and others waxed poetic regarding honey's virtues as good physical and fiscal medicine. Romans greeted their guests with honey saying, "Here is honey which the gods provide for your health. It is the elixir of life. Partake."

The Bible mentions honey or honeycomb more than forty times. It's noted in Luke 24:42 that after Christ rose from the dead, the first food he ate was "broiled fish and honeycomb."

The bee species we are familiar with is *Apis mellifera*, which means "bringing honey." The name indicates that men first thought that bees carried honey from the flowers to the hive. It was only later that men understood that bees actually made honey at home.

Did the bee train the plants to supply nectar, or did the flowering blossom seduce the bee into proxy-sex with every pollen-laden plant on the block? If you enjoy investigating nature's mysteries, you should read *The Botany of Desire: A Plant's Eye View of the World*, which explores the notion that bees and plants have evolved to satisfy humankind's most basic yearnings, and asks the question, who is domesticating whom?

VITAMIN BEE

After decades of turning up its nose at this ancient remedy, modern medicine's turning sweet on honey. Research shows that honey is antimicrobial due to its very high sugar content, low pH, and the presence of organic acids, which makes it ideal for treating cuts, scrapes, and burns and preventing scarring.

Honey's high carbohydrate content makes it a terrific source of energy. It contains vital minerals such as calcium, copper, iron, magnesium, manganese, phosphorous, potassium, sodium, and zinc, and it's also chockfull of niacin, B6, thiamin, riboflavin, and pantothenic acid. See what you miss on a low-carb diet? Open your mind along with your mouth.

But sweetest of all, honey is full of natural antioxidants, which protect us from free-radical stress. However, as with most foods, the less the honey is processed, the more antioxidants it has. Unfiltered, dark honey has the highest content.

In the past, diabetics were advised to avoid not only sugar, but honey also. However, we now know that it's the amount of carbohydrates, not the *type*, that has to be monitored. Therefore, honey may be included in a diabetic diet as long as physician's instructions are followed and blood sugar levels are controlled.

Frankly, honey is all about sex. No, not what you're thinking. It's that those wacky, busy little bees perform more than 80 percent of all crop pollination in America—and one-third of our food supply is the result of bee pollination.

Honey is produced through a symbiotic process between the queen, drones, and worker bees, along with the supporting cast—those horny, pollen-laden flowers. It's a very hard-working, well-organized relationship—just like your own community—where insects and flowers work toward a common goal: to perpetuate the species.

That being said, let's get cooking. Here are some tips: When substituting honey for granulated sugar in recipes for baked goods, use half the amount. For example if a recipe calls for one cup of sugar, use a half-cup of honey. Its high fructose content gives honey a higher sweetening power than sugar. Also, reduce the amount of liquid in the recipe by one-fourth cup for each cup of honey used and add about a half-teaspoon of baking soda for each cup of honey.

Honey adds a sweet, smooth, and distinctive taste to recipes. It also absorbs and retains moisture, which retards the drying-out and staling of baked goods.

Store honey at room temperature. If it crystallizes, don't freak out. Simply remove the lid and place the container in hot water until the crystals dissolve, or microwave it for 30 seconds or so until the crystals dissolve. If you nuke it, don't overdo, and check it carefully along the way, or you'll end up with a melt-down.

WHAT'S WITH A HONEYMOON?

With my indefatigable Aquarian curiosity pushing me, I just had to find out about the origin of the term "honeymoon." Here's what I discovered: In ancient Babylon, about four thousand years ago, for a month after the wedding the bride's father would supply his son-in-law with all the mead he could drink (mead is a wine made from honey). Because the Babylonian calendar was lunar based, this period was called the "honey month"—or "honeymoon." Traditionally, after the honeymoon concluded, the bride and groom would consume the traditional "honeymoon salad"— lettuce alone with no dressing.

From a vegetarian point of view, it's consoling to know that honey is the only natural food made without destroying any kind of life. It is also the only food produced by insects that is eaten by humans!

Life is short. Be ever attentive to whatever glorious treat the earth will offer up today. The sound of the wind rustling through the trees, clouds gilt-edged with the setting sun, birds hovering then descending to snatch up a tasty morsel . . . and busy, buzzing bees flourishing in their wondrous world that many of us take for granted. Nevermore!

So, bee happy! Bee healthy! Bee nice to a bee—and eat your honey.

"Liquid Candy"

THE COLD HARD TRUTHS ABOUT SOFT DRINKS

Missy nonchalantly glances around the empty school cafeteria, then spots her connection. She feels the gnawing, the craving, the crash, and her body needs a boost . . . now! She digs deep into her lint-lined pocket and pulls out a crumpled dollar bill. Fingers trembling, she is barely able to slip the bill into the slot. But she does, and with a thud, out pops her fix. She hurriedly cracks it open and imbibes deeply. She savors the substance, feeling her energy returning and confident that her "fix" will be enough to keep her alert at least through recess.

Missy is six years old.

Vernor's ginger ale is my hallucinogenic flashback machine.

The first soda pop made in the U.S., Vernor's ginger ale was created in Detroit, Michigan, in 1866. As youngsters in the 1950s, my siblings and I attended a summer church camp in Ohio, where my grandfather was district superintendent. Our large family bunked in Papaw's classic pink and brown lake house on a channel facing the muddy, catfish-filled Lake St. Mary's, but it was like vacationing on the Atlantic Ocean as far as we were concerned. Pure, innocent childhood bliss and joy.

In the center of the wooded church campground stood a smoky, cinderblock canteen that belched out charbroiled burger-and-fries fumes. We'd pester Dad for some change, then purchase all-day suckers and golden glass bottles of ice-cold, forehead-numbing Vernor's. Nirvana! Back then, if not for the discipline of my parental units, we would've gladly consumed it at every meal, and then some. Darn my parents—they made us sit up straight, mind our manners, go to church, eat fruits and veggies, and drink fresh juice, milk, and water, with only an occasional pitcher of Kool-Aid.

Back when I was a kid, soft drinks were considered a reward, a special treat, which if not handled equitably, could cause war between siblings. My brothers and I would line up the glasses and evenly split a bottle of soda three ways, and, God forbid, if one us got more than the other, the fur would fly!

So what's the big deal now with drinking sodas?

I'll tell you. In the last twenty years, the consumption rate of soft drinks has risen 114 percent and snack foods a walloping 233 percent. The tooth fairy must be exhausted.

It sounds preposterous: Soft drinks, America's other drinking problem, are killing our children and grandchildren. The pandering enablers: Mom and Dad role models, TV, peer pressure, and predatory, "smart-bomb" advertising. Like the cigarette business, carbonated soft drink manufacturers are constantly searching for new markets, investing billions targeting our youth and our adult penchant for denial. According to a January 1999 article in *Beverage* magazine, "Influencing elementary schools is very important to the soft drink marketers." Soft drinks are nutritionally bankrupt, and caffeine is a socially acceptable form of speed, and sugar is essentially a legalized unregulated drug!

Carbonated drinks are the single most significant source of refined sugars in the American diet. Refined sugar, the white deceiver, and high-fructose corn syrup are foods that, according to research, create health problems. Sugar is so changed from its original plant form and so concentrated that it could actually be considered a drug. Just ten teaspoons (approximately the amount found in one soft drink) can temporarily immobilize the immune system by about 33 percent. Bottoms up!

Warnings about the dangers of soft drink consumption came to us as early as 1942 when the American Medical Association's Council on Food and Nutrition made the following statement: "From the health point of view, it is desirable especially to have restriction of such use of sugar as is represented by consumption of sweetened carbonated beverages and forms of candy, which are of low nutritional value. The Council believes it would be in the interest of the public health for all practical means to be taken to limit consumption of sugar in any form in which it fails to be combined with significant proportions of other foods of high nutritive quality."

Can you guesstimate how many tooth-rotting colas will be consumed worldwide during the next hour? An unfathomable 27 million, which translates to more than 600 million per day. And the average North American consumes the equivalent of nineteen teaspoons of sugar every day, mostly in processed food and beverages.

Furthermore, soft drinks could be considered a true witch's brew with ingredients and additives often including Aspartame (thought to be a potent neurotoxin and endocrine disrupter), refined white sugar, sucrose, corn syrup, caffeine (a powerful diuretic and stimulant), brominated vegetable oils, food colorings, caramel colorings, and yummy phosphoric acid to give the drinks their "bite." Phosphoric acid is associated with calcium loss and kidney stones according to *Alternative Medicine* (Burton Goldberg Group, p. 942). It befuddled me why anyone would put oil into a cola so I check out the FDA and their take on brominated vegetable oil. BVO, mostly found in citrus soft drinks (read your labels), such as Code Red Mountain Dew, has been allowed in our foods since 1977 but remains in the top two thousand toxicity additives and must be reexamined every six months. Like PCBs, BVO leaves traces in the fat cells of your body. Bromine itself is defined as a heavy, volatile, corrosive, reddish-brown liquid element that emits a highly irritating vapor. It is used in producing gasoline, antiknock mixtures, fumigants, dyes, and photographic chemicals. All this to keep the flavor oil from separating in your precious soda. Bleah!

Then there's the caffeine. Extreme caffeine intake can cause rapid heartbeat, elevated blood pressure, constriction of the blood vessels to the brain, along with aggression and recklessness. *That sounds like symptoms of road rage, doesn't it?*

Another lovely ingredient in colas is caramel colorings, which have genetic effects and are suspected carcinogens. Often, polyethylene glycol is used as an ingredient; it's also used in antifreeze as an oil solvent. On a positive note, though, next time you're stuck in a snow or ice storm, grab a cola and pour it on your windshield.

Heavy metals get into soft drinks because the phosphoric acid in them can leach the aluminum from the cans they come in. The industry claims to have solved the problem by plastic-coating the interiors of the cans, but nevertheless, toxic amounts can still leach into the beverage. There is a widespread theory that heavy metals can be deposited in the brain and bones and perhaps is implicated as contributing to Alzheimer's disease.

In recent years, soft drinks have been overall market winners. Americans drink more than 13 billion gallons of kidney-straining, immune-suppressing, tooth-rotting sodas each year. Researcher Michael F. Jacobson, Ph.D., suggests individuals and families should consider how much soda they drink and reduce consumption accordingly. Dutiful parents should stock their homes with natural, healthful foods and beverages for their family members to enjoy. Doctors should routinely ask their patients how much soda they drink and advise them of better dietary habits.

But what about Missy and other children like her who are

hooked on soda? School systems nowadays seem to auction themselves off to the highest bidder (as do other organizations catering to our children); they should stop hawking soft drinks, candy, and similar foods in cafeteria vending machines. Food and drink in schools should profit the students' health, not the administration's bottom line. I'm dismayed that anyone with morals and ethics would market such unhealthy food to our children. Shame on them!

Urban Tumbleweeds

AMERICA'S LOVE AFFAIR WITH LITTERING

The after-supper sunset strolls my wife and I take with our thirteen-year-old dog, Annie, are our way to throttle down from the day's activities, soak in nature's beauty, and bond. As we grow older together, we've learned to gaze upward in order to not miss the clusters of buzzing insects swirling against the blue sky, breeze-fueled leaf cyclones, chittering squirrels, and towering thunderheads piled on the horizon, bronze sunbeams slicing through them.

One evening, as we watched bats darting about enjoying their evening meal of gnats and mosquitoes, a noisy pack of skateboarding "dudes and dudettes" whizzed by, wantonly lobbing half-eaten burger and fry containers, barely missing my wife, but nailing me upside the head. Annie snarled as leftover Mountain Dew bottles skittered to a stop amid the greasy wrappers floating around like "urban tumbleweeds." The hooligans skated away, hooting and laughing derisively, adding to the mess as the orange sparks of their discarded cigarette butts hit the cooling pavement.

In a flash, I retro'd to the 1970s TV commercial of the "sad Indian" watching people litter with carefree abandon and shedding a tear for the lack of respect for our planet. It seems that many of us have forgotten that we are stewards of the earth and that we belong to it, not the other way around. Several generations have been lost to environmental apathy, clueless that their individual

and collective actions harm earth's delicate ecology and ultimately our families' health, or the lack thereof.

Regrettably, some people were never taught how to behave by their parents, and they now seem unable to learn. Litterbugs aren't necessarily bad people, just thoughtless, immature, selfish, ignorant, or "il-litter-ate." Littering is their way of giving the world the proverbial "finger." It's a super-caffeinenated Mountain Dew mentality.

It seems that the people most likely to not "get it" and make a habit of littering are those between sixteen and twenty-four years old who are single, smoke, and eat fast food at least twice a week. Their reasoning will astound you: "I wasn't aware I was littering, and besides, I don't care. Others will pick up after me."

But before you become too judgmental, hold on a minute. Admit it—aren't we all at least just a bit wasteful at times? Take last night's dinner, for example. Is there a similarity between blithely tossing good food into the garbage and wonton littering? Recycling assumes many faces. An ancient saying goes "to waste just a single grain of rice is a sin."

Use of leftovers is the great-grandmother of recycling, our first exposure to the concept. In times past, when food wasn't as easy to come by as it is today, it just made good economic sense not be wasteful. Early in my life, I discovered the foundation for recycling formulated in Mom's kitchen as she magically concocted fabulous suppers out of carefully managed leftovers. Anyone who lived during the great Depression can attest to the benefits of frugal, leftover cooking ideas. Taking the burden off the environment can begin at the supper table where we as a family can counteract the much larger political economics of pollution. Eat only what you need, and those scraps from meal preparation (no meat scraps, please!) can go into the compost pile to replenish and renourish the earth.

A multitude of dishes can be created out of recycled leftovers. If you were a mouse in a restaurant kitchen, you'd hear this behind the kitchen doors: "Hey, chef, we've reserved these savory, tasty

bits of meat crumbs from slicing the pot roast. Let's refrigerate them and we'll make vegetable beef soup for tomorrow's menu." Fried rice, corned beef hash, egg rolls, burritos, soups and stews, frittata, quiche, stir-fries, bread pudding, potato salad, hash browns, and rich, silky stocks are but a few recipes utilizing the remains of yesterday's menu. Good kitchen economics.

Recycling of both food and nonfood items provides American industry with an environmentally preferable source of raw materials, plus it saves energy, reduces greenhouse gas emissions and air and water pollutants. Recycling and not littering is great for our health and that of the planet. How humans choose to eat and waste has a directly proportional effect on controversial depletion of the earth's protective ozone layer. It's ripples in the pond, grasshopper.

If you subscribe to this philosophy, then you're already connecting the dots between dinner-table leftovers, littering, and recycling. Recycling makes good environmental and fiscal sense. How we deal with our family's or society's leftovers determines whether they are a plus or minus and whether the environment or humans win or lose.

At the grocery, it's simple to use our purchasing power by selecting items packaged in recyclable containers. We can begin reusing plastic containers, coffee cans, and glass jars for storing leftovers, kitchen hardware utensils, pencils, nails, chopsticks, pens, and work items. And always request paper bags at the grocery instead of plastic so your family can reuse them to package other recycling, such as newspapers. *Save a tree!*

Hey, wine connoisseurs! Recycling just one glass bottle can save enough energy to light a one hundred-watt bulb for twenty hours. And as you turn the pages of this book, keep in mind that one ton of recycled paper made by recycling uses 64 percent less energy, 50 percent less water, and 74 percent less air pollution, as well as saving seventeen trees and creating five times more jobs than the same amount of paper produced from virgin wood pulp. *Cheers!*

A majority of human-spawned garbage ends under those charming, mountainous landfills you see as you tool down America's highways. The garbage ferments and decomposes, rudely belching gases out of the vent pipes and chimneys that poke out of the mounds. Landfills aren't the only source of methane, though: Thirty to forty times a day, from one end or another, we all contribute this highly flammable gas into the atmosphere, if you get my drift. Who among us (okay, the guys anyway), during our mindless, reckless adolescence, didn't at least once attempt to ignite the emissions coming through our BVDs? Hanging in the air, however, was always the fear that one of these "blue flamers" might backfire and cause irreparable damage.

One evening, over the clatter of a sinkful of dinner dishes being washed, Mom thought she heard a muffled "flarp" sound coming from her son's bedroom. She halted and pulled off her Playtex gloves and yelled, "What are you boys doing in there? Tell Grant it's time for him to go home!"

"He's not here anymore," son Billy nervously replied.

"Yes he is. I just saw him go in there with you fifteen minutes ago," she said as she entered the darkened room in time to see a pair of smoking Spider-man underwear with a blown-out crotch float to the floor. Bug-eyed and sniffling, Billy explained. "Mommy, we were lighting our tooters, and Grant sneezed, burped, and hiccuped at the same time and . . . I . . . *waaaah* . . . blew Grant up!" *A miniature Hindenburg!*

As for the trash littering our roadways and sidewalks, fast food and junk food wrappers, food packaging and cans, along with beverage containers and cigarette butts are the major culprits. Personally, I equate fast food consumption with personal weakness: an inability and refusal to amend one's ways, even though a person may know it's the correct thing to do. Much of this trash could be contained through recycling instead of using up the earth's resources, but I often hear such contrary rationalisms as "The Good Book says to subdue and dominate the earth and take from it what

we need. I don't see any scripture that says we should recycle." A literalist cop out!

Sadly, we live in a disposable society where even helpless newborn infants are occasionally flung into Dumpsters, not to mention the millions of reckless folk tossing entire bags of gooey fast-food containers out of their car windows. Who do they think is going to clean up after them, their mothers? Perhaps the fast-food industry considers all that litter to be efficient advertising since their logos are plastered onto all that garbage on the roadsides.

Encourage your families to "give a hoot and don't pollute." In our collective minds and hearts, let's plant a loving dream of an America that's fresh, clean, and full of life, without a ciggy butt-strewn ecosystem full of mountains of decomposing garbage, acid rain, and fouled lakes and streams. I may be idealistic, but I believe that in order to clean up the planet and ensure our families' future welfare on it, our disposable society must begin by first cleaning itself. The process begins at home, where the heart is.

Ultimately, how much we contribute to the welfare of the earth depends on our own comfort levels. Recently, while watching the evening news, I became overwhelmed with the tribulations of the world. What could one person do to make a difference? Suddenly, it was clear as a bell: I feel powerful when dealing with the problems in my family, in my home, and in my own community. I lose all that power, however, when I try to cope with the world as a whole. Perhaps we are supposed to think globally and act locally; however, I have resigned myself to thinking locally and acting locally. It's better than not doing anything, and it's what keeps me sane.

Sex and Food

OR, EATING FOR PLEASURE

Ever since Adam and Eve—or was it Lilith?—waltzed through the Garden of Eden sharing a juicy apple, love affairs and food have gone hand in hand.

I adore food and love intimacy, but here's the big question: Is food better than sex? After all, if food is lousy, you don't have to lie to the chef, and food won't complain if you're not hungry.

Despite the disturbing mental imagery, as we get older, we can continue to have active and satisfying sex lives. For many, age only makes it better—like good wine and cheese. But were you aware of the influential roll food and nutrition plays in the success of a romantic interlude with your sweetheart?

According to our eloquent researchers at *Encyclopedia Britannica*: "[There is a] psycho-physiological reaction that a well-prepared meal can have upon the human organism. The combination of various sensuous reactions—the visual satisfaction of the sight of appetizing food, the olfactory stimulation of their pleasing smells and the tactile gratification afforded the oral mechanism by rich, savory dishes—tend to bring on a state of general euphoria conducive to sexual expression." *Took the words right out of my mouth.*

Since ancient times, humans have tried to boost their libidos with magic potions, fragrances, and a variety of exotic foods. Casanova downed oysters and a cup of chocolate before venturing into a lady's boudoir. Montezuma II consumed fifty glasses of

chocolate sweetened with honey to sustain his virility. Cleopatra seduced Mark Anthony in a scented royal chamber knee-deep in rose petals. (Ouch! Hope there weren't any thorns in there.) And it was believed that the spice cardamom, known as the "fire of Venus," has a magical affect on the opposite sex.

All of these are considered aphrodisiacs. The term aphrodisiac comes from "Aphrodite," the name of the Greek goddess of love. According to Richard Miller, author of *The Magical and Ritual Use of Aphrodisiacs*, aphrodisiacs should do one or more of the following: improve sexual health, increase sexual awareness, relax inhibitions, arouse sexual feelings by stimulating the nervous system, augment physical energy, help conquer impotence and frigidity, and strengthen the glands involved with sex.

Occasionally, Cupid needs help, especially if you've clogged up your plumbing by consuming all the wrong foods and beverages. Yes, if you expect to "rise" to the occasion, food can positively or negatively affect your performance. It's all about blood flow and circulation, folks. Therefore, any foods that would be bad for the heart would conversely thwart your sexual performance. The same fats that clog your arteries are the same fats that clog blood flow to the nether regions, therefore diminishing your performance.

According to Dr. Cynthia Watson, author of *A Guide to Aphrodisiacs and Sexual Pleasure*, a well-balanced diet, replete with fresh vegetables, fruits, and lean sources of protein, supplies essential nutrients for good sexual performance.

So, let's talk about some of these good foods, beginning with everyone's favorite, chocolate. There are many delicious points to be addressed in the defense of chocolate. For one thing, it feels so wonderfully seductive in the mouth. According to Deralee Scanlon, R.D., chocolate's reputation as an aphrodisiac may be due to its abundant supply of phenylethylamine, an amphetamine-like chemical. (For example, our phenylethylamine levels go up when we meet "the right person.") Chocolate also contains caffeine, which stimulates the release of epinephrine, one of the neural messengers that triggers sexual response. Large doses of cocoa are believed to

stimulate the production of the neurotransmitter serotonin, which in turn gives us the sensation of being in love.

Avocados, besides being storehouses of beneficial nutrients such as potassium, phosphorous, sulphur, magnesium and other minerals, are credited with supplying energy and desire for sex.

The ancient Greeks believed carrots, or "philons," as they called them, had aphrodisiac power. Carrots supply an estrogen-like compound that stimulates the sexual appetite. Plus, eating carrots help you see in the dark bedroom. The Greeks also considered figs a sensual favorite. Figs contain magnesium, which is essential for producing sex hormones and improving your eyesight.

The apple we referred to earlier from the Garden of Eden not only tastes good, but it is visually suggestive: when it is cut open down the middle, it displays a seed pattern suggesting female genitalia. And the pomegranate, highly praised by D. H. Lawrence in *Woman in Love*, has been touted as an aphrodisiac since Old Testament writings.

Hot peppers stimulate circulation, and good circulation means good physical response to an outside sexual stimulation. Shiitake mushrooms are known to have a positive effect on sexual strength in men and a stimulating effect in females. Garlic was widely used in ancient times among the Egyptians, Greeks, and the Romans. The "stinking rose" is alleged to contain compounds related to sex hormones. (Pass the mints, please.)

And finally, drink plenty of good, fresh, filtered water.

Which foods are bad for good sex? During my many years as a maitre d', I prepared countless tableside dinners for lovers. Over those years I found the perennial favorite romantic dinner of all times is—drum roll please—a glass of Borolo, fettuccini Alfredo, Caesar salad, and a big, juicy, inch-thick, rare steak, followed by the crunchy-topped, satin-like crème brûlée. Sounds romantic, but in fact it is a prelude to disaster.

Those macho hunks of steak and other red meats may be considered sexy; however, we now know that the saturated fats those well-marbled cuts of meat can clog our arteries. Fatty foods in general require a lot of energy to digest, which is why we get sleepy after a big, heavy meal and want to nap. Much of the blood flows to the stomach to assist in digestion, when it could be better pulsing somewhere else.

Some foods are marginally bad. For example, butter is better—in moderation—than margarine, but olive oil is by far the best. Use the fruity extra virgin first cold pressed olive oil for salad dressing and bread dipping, and use all-purpose olive oil for baking and frying.

And those glasses of wine or other alcohol you slurped down likely just make you *think* you are a good lover, so practice moderation. Illicit street drugs may give you the impression you are a superstud, but they're a bummer. And above all, avoid smoking—before and after sex!—and cut down on your sugar intake.

Last, but not least, don't forget to accompany your good diet with regular exercise, which is paramount for increased sexual prowess as it tones, strengthens, and increases endurance. (In fact, the sex act itself is an excellent aerobic exercise.) Exercise increases intra-cellular oxygenation, releases tons of endorphins, slightly lowers LDL (the "bad" cholesterol), increases estrogen production in women (especially in menopause) and testosterone in both genders, helps regulate menstrual cycles, and increases the production of adrenal hormones.

I must share with you a recent epiphany. It dawned on me why men who lack regular sexual intimacy have more wrinkles around their eyes. I can only assume it's caused by their frequently having to beg, "Can we, can we, please, please . . . tonight?"

The next time you feel the tingling for romance, remember that the right food sets the stage for seduction. Plus it doesn't hurt to be in love with the right person.

Now, stiffen up, and save a few bucks by calling the pharmacy and canceling that Viagra prescription.

Tea

THE CIVILIZED BEVERAGE

Ever observe a restaurant customer who reaches into a pocket or purse, brings out a tea bag, and asks for only a pot of hot water? Nerdy, you say? Over my years of slinging hash, tea drinkers were mutually considered pains in the, well . . . tea bag, since serving a "proper" cup of tea requires more attention than does simply topping off a cup of coffee. The bag needs tending, and the water needs to be kept hot and frequently topped off. Then one day I found myself saying, "Miss, where's the lemon? Couldn't you warm the cup with a bit of hot water first?" The waitress rolled her eyes. I flushed and realized, just like in a cheap B horror flick, that I'd become one of "them"—a needy, nerdy tea elitist.

Everywhere I go, well-meaning friends wisecrack regarding my ubiquitous mug o' tea. Tea is my equivalent of a cuppa joe, a diet soda, or an alcoholic beverage. I call it my longevi-tea. Admittedly, I am a tea junkie. The word "snob" sounds too harsh. After all, tea is my best friend. If I'm cold, it warms me; if I'm too hot, it cools me. If I'm depressed, it cheers me; and if I'm excited, it calms me. Like one of the family. Tea touches our souls. Tea is a ceremony in itself, a stand-up performance in simplicity.

I seem to remember Mick Jagger crooning that "everyone needs a little tea and sympathy." What shall we sing about in this new millennium? I daresay if the major powers that be sat down together to a soothing cup of tea, our precariously teetering world

could be at peace. Charles Dickens summed it up, more or less, when he wrote: "My dear, if you could give me a cup of tea to clear my muddle of a head, I should better understand your affairs."

However, Dickens wasn't writing about green tea. In fact, just a few short years ago, if you had mentioned specifically green tea to the average tea drinker in the U.K., Europe, or North America, the response probably would have been "Green tea? What's that?"

WE'RE NUMBER 2! WE'RE NUMBER 2!

Known as one of China's great treasures, tea is second only to water as a world beverage. Over five thousand years ago, Chinese emperor and herbalist Shen Nung was undoubtedly double-dipping his dumpling in the spicy chile oil when he bumped against his tea bush causing a leaf to fall into his small pot of boiling water. Ergo, the first cup of tea, a refreshingly healthy beverage. Buddhist monks are believed to have brought tea to Japan in 552 A.D. But it was more than a thousand years later, in 1667, that tea was introduced to jolly old England when Thomas Garway sold it at his coffee house in London's Exchange Ally. And what patriotic American could forget the Boston Tea Party of 1773, which led to American independence.

So maybe those "nerdy" tea drinkers are a tad fussier than the average diner, perhaps, for good reasons.

THE FRENCH PARADOX: TEA DRINKERS AND HEART DISEASE

The French are not the only ones with bragging rights to their own paradox. Add the Japanese too, as Lester Mitscher, Ph.D. hints in his outstanding book, *The Green Tea Book*, (Avery Publishing

Group, NY, NY) "Despite a high percentage of smokers (75 percent of adult men), Japan has an astonishingly low rate of heart disease. It seems possible that the polyphenols in green tea cause the same paradox as polyphenols in red wine. The French Paradox results from the fact that the French outlive Americans and suffer significantly fewer heart attacks, despite the fact that smoking is a national pastime and the French diet is swimming in saturated fat." Alas, Europe is becoming rapidly westernized in the fast food arena, and thus is beginning to suffer from the same, well-documented, degenerative diseases that plague junk-food-addicted Americans.

WOULD YOU LIKE TEA WITH THAT SOYBURGER?

An encouraging Japanese epidemiology study came to the conclusion that drinking eight to ten cups tea per day can positively affect cholesterol levels, even if you smoke, drink, or are overweight. Fill the kettle. It won't be *too long* until you're drinking *oolong*.

Other studies have shown an apparent reduction in the risk of cardiovascular disease among healthy people who drink tea on a regular basis, which also applies to all of us who have already experienced heart problems and fear reoccurrence.

What's the connection? Tea contains the same excellent class of nutrients and polyphenols one finds in red wine and cocoa. Polyphenols are antioxidants believed to negate the effects of a fatty diet and smoking. *Want a light?*

One caveat: As with alcohol and driving, tea and cow's milk or cream straight from the fridge don't mix well, because it's been discovered that milk proteins muddle the magical healing properties of tea. So if you insist on adding dairy to your tea, use scalded milk, not cream. Green tea stands alone.

Thankfully, green tea now is showing up in restaurants. How-

ever, black and oolong teas are just as good since they also provide isoflavones and flavonoids, both very powerful antioxidants.

Dorothy Moore of Purdue University's School of Consumer and Family Sciences says that drinking at least four cups of green tea a day could provide enough active compounds to slow and prevent the growth of cancer cells. Think about it: cancer prevention in a teacup for the entire family, even the dog.

My dentist noticed that my family's cavity frequency dramatically decreased. So when I read that black or green tea, hot or cold, aids digestion, is antibacterial, and contain anti-aging properties, we had our explanation. Once a day, I slush the green tea around my mouth, as I would a mouthwash, becoming a bacterial mass-murderer. In an article in *The Dental Clinics of North America*, Dr, Michael Bral of the NYU College of Dentistry writes that the ideal anti-plaque agents in tea can eliminate disease-causing bacteria, reduce plaque and gingivitis, does not lead to the development of resistant bacteria, and is easy to use. *Natural Health* magazine recently reported that green tea (Camelilia sinensis) contains catechins that kill the bacteria in the mouth that form plaque (that sticky, cavity-causing gunk that your dentist has to scrape off). Catechins also wipe out the bacteria that cause bad breath.

TEA-ING IS BELIEVING

Delicately malty, smoky, full-bodied, and aromatic green or black teas come from the leaves of the same tree. Although the tree can grow over thirty feet tall, it is cut short like a bush so that the leaves can be easily plucked when harvested.

For centuries, woodsy green tea has been produced from leaves that laborers handled gently and heated soon after harvesting, as opposed to black tea leaves which are vigorously rolled to make

them release a particular enzyme, then left to sit for a few hours, during which time the enzymes interact with oxygen causing the leaves to develop a heartier flavor and a darker hue.

So the next time you stand at the coffee counter, bewildered by the overwhelming variety of pop coffees, simplify and opt for tea, the smart beverage. Become a healthy snob.

Tea, which began as a medicine and grew into a beverage, moved eighth-century Chinese author Lu Yu to pick up his quill to write of it: "Its liquor is like the sweetest dew from Heaven."

If you look into the bottom of your cup, the tea leaves will tell you that yesterday's legends are fast becoming today's healthy facts.

Soy

Is It the Perfect Food, or Does Tofu Have an Evil Twin?

What's square, white, weighs about eight ounces, jiggles, can make you gag, and often can clear a room in ten seconds?

The answer is, tofu, or soy bean curd. This much-maligned product has been known to strike dread in the hearts of the bravest culinary souls, paralyzing them in fear at its mere mention. (Not wholly unlike the feeling you might get when receiving notification of an IRS audit.)

Flash back to the flower children of the mid and late 1960s, when a rumor wafted through the grease-filled air that the Golden Arches folks used a sinister form of fibrous soybeans as filler in their burgers. "Ai-ee! Hack! P-tooey! We've been poisoned!" In retrospect, what we should have protested instead was the saturated-fat-laden bovine tallow used to deep-fry those golden brown, salt-covered french fries. (Just as an FYI, though, McDonalds and Taco Bell have indeed been using soy products as filler for decades. Nevertheless, don't expect to see the International House of Bean Curd popping up in your 'hood soon.)

New findings are out about tofu and soy products, however, and as I painfully sift through the mountains of information on the subject, I have to ask myself, "Is it actually—gasp!—*bad* for us?" In my catering production kitchen, I'm often referred to as "The Tofu King." And since I've consumed and prepared just about everything imaginable from tofu and related soy products, the idea that it might be harmful is the *last* thing I want to hear. After decades of aggressive research and marketing and touting the wiggly curd as a miracle cure-all for many of humanity's maladies, I wonder, alas, is the honeymoon over? Tell me it ain't so!

Is mass tofu-phobia justified? Can tofu really make your brain shrivel and encourage dementia and breast cancer? What's with that? For a substance that has been providing nourishment for humans for so many years, this Rodney Dangerfield of food is getting no respect.

But what I'm placing in your to-go bag is whether we should be alarmed about these new studies regarding the safety of eating tofu, or is this junk science? Is it safe to continue making tofu a foundation of our diet? Ignorance may be bliss, but information is a powerful tool, so let's look objectively at both sides of the issue, and, as my Mom would have said, "Don't throw the baby out with the bath water." We need to encourage more funding for further studies and season our own judgment with a generous helping of knowledge.

When I asked about the validity of tofu-phobia, the Indiana Soybean Board responded passionately with this reassurance: "Wendell, I think the important thing is that overreacting and taking things out of context is the biggest problem . . . Asians have been eating soy foods for centuries and undoubtedly there is no evidence that they have less cognitive function."

So how many centuries have people been eating tofu? Tradition has it that tofu was invented by Liu An (179–122 B.C.), a prince of the Han Dynasty, supposedly while searching for a substance to help him achieve immortality. But way before then, in 2838 B.C., Chinese Emperor Cheng Nung developed soy cultivation. Soybeans did not, however, grace American soil until Samuel Bowen brought it to the continent and Henry Yonge planted the first soy crop on his farm in Thunderbolt, Georgia, in 1765. Did Henry know when he

sowed the seeds of soy he would be saving us from the sorrow of serious sickness and senility? *Somebody let a snake loose?*

FERMENTED VERSUS UNFERMENTED

Certain types of fermented foods are actually very good for our gastrointestinal tracts, helping to keep points A through Z in good working order, which is imperative to achieve optimum health. Soybeans are among those foods that are best whether fresh or fermented.

Indianapolis health guru Deb McClure-Smith of Good Earth Whole Foods pointed out to me that fermented soy products such as tempeh and miso are much easier for our Earth Suits to digest than processed silken tofu products.

Tempeh, a fermented soybean product that comes in cakes, is made from whole soybeans and has a nutty, smoky flavor and is similar to mushrooms in texture. At my home we us it to cook sloppy joes, barbecue, Cajun "steaks," spaghetti sauce, taco filling, and chili. The grandkids love it, and sneaky chef that I am, I don't tell them how good it is for them!

Four ounces of cooked tempeh contains 17 grams of protein, a mere 204 calories, 15 grams of carbohydrates, and 8 grams of (good) fat. Plus, it's full of calcium, iron, zinc, and fiber. It's so much better for you than the same size portion of steak, and doesn't contain the heart-damaging saturated fats, antibiotics, and growth hormones so commonly found in "mad cow" beef.

A plethora of reasons to make soy the center of our diets abounds. In 2001 in San Diego, California, at the Fourth International Symposium on the Role of Soy in Preventing and Treating Chronic Disease, a mutually agreed-upon conclusion was reached:

Soy foods may reduce the risk of heart disease; prostate, colon and breast cancers; and osteoporosis and osteoarthritis. Soy foods may even help lower blood pressure, prevent renal problems in diabetics, and improved cognitive function.

Wait a minute. Did they say "cognitive function"?

"Yes," said the Indiana Soybean Board. "Soy may possibly have a positive effect on cognitive function. Two preliminary research studies presented at the symposium showed that soy actually improved several aspects of cognitive function, especially verbal memory. Hopefully, this good news will alleviate any concerns you've had about that pesky soy-and-dementia issue. The Soy Board reminds people to keep things in perspective. The negative effects were found only in an epidemiological study; however, animal studies suggest just the opposite—soy has beneficial effects on cognitive function."

This is somewhat contrary with what Dr. Lon Wright of the Pacific Health Research Institute presents. He has conducted a study of 3,734 middle-aged Japanese-American men that indicates that eating tofu more than twice a week may be linked to dementia. White's theory is that the phytoestrogens in tofu interfere with the brain's estrogen receptors and keep the brain from properly using estrogen. His article appeared in an edition of the *Journal of the American College of Nutrition*. But listen to this: He says, "I would be violating a cardinal rule if I said my data says you shouldn't eat tofu [or other soy foods]." *Ah-hah!* White emphasizes this data can't be turned into sweeping conclusions, and the findings must be considered preliminary. And according to Beverly Creamer, staff writer for a Honolulu advertiser newspaper, "It's the first time scientists have labeled a dietary risk factor for the disease that affects 2 percent of the nation's sixty-five-year-olds and up to 16 percent of eighty-year-olds." Very interesting!

Finally, White's study was based on *processed* tofu, which is not fermented, and which could be considered another endorsement for the fermented forms of the bean or edamame.

Here's more spice for the health stew: University of Minnesota

scientist Mindy Kurzer, Ph.D., who does extensive research on the humble bean, assures us that there are no data connecting soy and cancer. "There is a theoretical risk that *processed* soy might promote breast cancer in some way," Kurzer added, "but it's purely theoretical at this point."

All this information is making my brain hurt!

Alternative medicine guru Dr. Andrew Weil believes "soy foods such as edamame, tofu, tempeh, and soy milk are much more likely to help you than hurt you. Therefore, I recommends one to two servings per day, even to women with breast cancer." That's about 40 mg of risk-free, tasty isoflavonoids. Weil does not advise using soy supplements because of their high isoflavone content and lack of evidence demonstrating their long-term safety. Forget the "for suckers only" designer fad foods laced with soy isoflavonoids. Instead, Weil suggests discovering the delightful edamame (which means "beans on branches"), a soybean harvested while still green and at the peak of ripening, just before it reaches the hardened stage.

Perhaps the problem is simply our American lifestyle. Otherwise -healthy Asians who come to live in America ultimately succumb to the same health maladies as we native-borns. Is it the fluoridated water, the pesticides, food coloring, preservatives, fungicides on our produce, or our overly polluted environment? Or is it the change in eating habits?

All I ask is that you take the negative findings with a grain of sea salt until all of the research is in. Until then, open your mind as well as your mouth to the healthy *virtues* of *unprocessed* soy products available on the grocers' shelves. Opt for healthful, unprocessed soy products; but as with any food or drink, don't go overboard and follow the American mantra, "More is better." Most of the time, less is more.

Will someone pass me the soy nuts, please?

There's a Fungus Among Us!

SHIITAKES: THE HEART-SMART FOOD OF THE FUTURE

Bathed in the hazy early morning sun, Gordon reverently pauses to witness nature weaving her wonderful, mysterious web.

Wiping the sleep from his eyes, he takes a sip of coffee, and, as is his habit, mentally counts out the forty steps from the front porch to his mushroom logs nestled deep in the undulating hills of his Brown County, Indiana, farm. Out of the corner of his eye he catches sight of a cloud drifting through the windless back meadow. "What's causing that smoke?" he wonders. "Has someone over there got a campfire going?" Soon, though, he realizes that the cloud isn't smoke, but a fog of mushroom spores looking for a place to settle down, grow, and reproduce.

THE SUBJECT OF GREAT FASCINATION

Mushrooms were once the stuff of folklore. The ancient Egyptians considered them the sons of gods, sent to earth riding thunderbolts. In medieval times, the Celts thought they were

merely umbrellas for pixies and elves, and that they had to be gathered under a full moon to be edible.

Mushrooms are one of the more popular food items going these days, and not just the white moonlight mushrooms. My favorite is the noble shiitake, which, with its marvelous healing powers, has for more than two thousand years been coveted as the finest edible mushroom in Asia. Now, Americans are catching on to this nutritional fungus. After all, five billion Chinese can't be wrong.

Commonly called Chinese black forest mushrooms, the Japanese word "shiitake" (pronounced *shee-tah-kee*) means literally "mushrooms from the shii tree" because they were originally cultivated on the Japanese evergreen oak called shii. So, if you want to pretend you are intelligent, remind someone when he or she says "shiitake mushrooms" they are being redundant.

Almost everyone has eaten shiitakes; they are those little dark brown slivers of mushrooms found in your favorite Asian take-out. The mushrooming popularity of this tasty fungus is partially due to its distinctive, woodsy flavor, and firm, meaty texture, which make them a delectable addition to practically any recipe. Shiitakes *(Lentinula edodes)* have much more flavor than the standard button or white mushrooms with which we are all accustomed.

An inaccurate assumption has long been held that mushrooms have no nutritional value, but au contraire, cherie: Despite the fact that shiitakes are 83 percent water, they are loaded with potassium, manganese, iron, copper, niacin, and vitamins A, B1, B2, C, D, and E. They also contain the essential amino acids found in meat, milk, and eggs, but without the calories and saturated fats. Four average-size shiitake mushrooms contain a mere 40 calories but pack around 10.3 grams of carbohydrate, 1.5 grams of fiber, 1.12 grams of protein, and a whopping 17.8 mcg selenium. Shiitakes are now one of the more popular sources of protein in Japan, China, and around the Pacific Rim.

Mushrooming interest in fungi

Fungi differ from plants and animals in that they can't produce their own energy; instead they absorb their nutrients from their environment. However, it's not a one-sided existence: fungi tap into living tree roots and absorb carbohydrates, and in return give the tree some much-needed minerals.

The Chinese have used shiitakes as a mainstay for their medicine for thousands of years, believing that the mushrooms dispel hunger, alleviate colds, and nourish the circulatory system. According to mushroom experts at Garuda International, Inc., "shiitake and other mushrooms have no green pigments (chlorophyll), they cannot make food from sunlight as do other plants but must live by eating plants or animals. Shiitakes favorite entree is a dead, hardwood tree." Garuda continues by sharing that "it is the shiitake's medicinal possibilities that are getting worldwide attention. Over the last two decades, scientists have isolated substances from shiitake that may play a role in the cure and prevention of modern civilization's dreaded illness of heart disease, cancer, viruses, bacteria, and AIDS." The therapeutic mushroom is also alleged to possess abilities to promote immune function, reduce inflammation, combat allergies, help balance sugar levels and supports our Earth Suits' detoxification mechanisms. This is even more validation that food is medicine.

Cooking and storage tips

Shiitakes are perfect additions to beans, rice, stir-fries, and pasta dishes, but they also make great sauces for fish and chicken. Throw them into an omelet or your next batch of homemade soup. As more farmers take up growing these previously hard to find and somewhat pricey 'shrooms, they can be purchased at a reasonable price from most grocery stores.

Fresh shiitakes should be firm, with spongy caps and small stems. Store them in the fridge in a brown paper bag rather than plastic, which would deprive them of oxygen and turn them into slime. They'll keep for about fourteen days.

To prepare fresh mushrooms, clean them thoroughly to remove any soil residue, remove the stems (you can reserve those to add flavor to a soup or stock), and slice the mushrooms thinly.

With dried mushrooms, first reconstitute them in hot water or wine. Don't throw away the soaking liquid, as it also is a marvelous addition to soups and sauces; however, you should strain the liquid through a sieve to eliminate any sediment from the soaking process. If you don't plan to use the mushroom juice immediately, it will freeze quite nicely.

Proper cooking really brings out the flavor of these fun fungi. Sauté them in a good, unhydrogenated oil, such as olive or peanut, or steam them in a scant amount of liquid such as water or wine in a tightly covered pan for about fifteen minutes. Now they're ready to be added to your dish of choice.

It all boils down to the fact that mushrooms are great food, and I can't think of any reason not to add shiitakes to one's culinary repertoire. So get your culinary show on the road and commence livening up your menus and protecting your family and their health by making shiitakes one of their dietary staples.

Garlic

LET'S MAKE A STINK OUT OF THIS ISSUE

As a bona fide garlic gastronome, I sincerely hope there is garlic in the hereafter, because that's what I'll be thereafter.

Around this beautiful world, for more than four thousand years, everyone's been making a big to-do about the innumerable, well-documented virtues of garlic. Homer praised it, and in ancient Egypt, fifteen pounds of the fresh bulb would purchase a healthy male slave. Sacrificial lambs of China three thousand years ago were seasoned with garlic to render them more acceptable to the gods. From the Greek historian Herodotus we learn that the workers constructing the Great Pyramids at Giza lived mainly on garlic and onions, allegedly to increase their stamina, went on strike and "copped an attitude" when deprived of the daily ration of garlic. Darned those garlic unions!

That must have been an open-minded civilization, whereas in modern times, we would deem the pungent aroma our bodies emit after eating garlic socially unacceptable. As the scholars imply, we need to learn from history, loosen up a little and smell the heavenly garlic. After all, if we were all on the same page and eating garlic regularly, no one would notice. Furthermore, in our all-too-busy and stressful lives, we could learn something from those ancient Egyptians who formulated what could perhaps be an early version of Prozac: a combination of camphor, valerian, and garlic-fermented wine.

To Smell to high heaven-ly?

In *A Midsummer Night's Dream*, Shakespeare wrote, "Eat no onions nor garlic, for we are to utter sweet breath."

Could it be that one man's stink is another man's perfume? Perhaps. But we shouldn't let the prospect of bad breath keep us from the amazing health benefits garlic has to offer.

In ancient Greece and Rome garlic was used to repel scorpions, treat dog bites and bladder infections, and cure leprosy and asthma. In the Middle Ages it was thought to prevent plague. In my efforts to keep her as healthy as possible, my twelve-year-old dog Annie gets raw garlic in her food everyday.

Christopher Ranch Garlic brand, a major player in the garlic industry, claims that the Vikings and Phoenicians packed garlic in their sea chests for long voyages, and in Boccaccio's *Decameron* a love-stricken young man sent garlic to his lady in order to win her heart—and he did. Never underestimate the power of love and garlic. Must've been a long-distance relationship.

Our good buddy, Louis Pasteur, in 1858, reported what modern research has confirmed: Garlic kills bacteria. Penicillin and sulfa drugs were hard to come by during World War II, so garlic was used as an antiseptic to disinfect open wounds and prevent gangrene.

Garlic can decrease the risk of cancer and heart disease, possibly lower cholesterol levels, reduce blood pressure, and strengthen the immune system and prevent infection. According to *Prescription for Nutritional Healing*, "garlic is also effective against fungal infections, including athletes foot, systemic candidiasis and yeast vaginitis, and there is some evidence that it may also destroy certain viruses, such as those associated with fever blisters, genital herpes, a form of the common cold, smallpox and a type of influenza." Garlic also has antioxidant properties, which are effective protections against oxidation and free radical stress. Garlic may also prevent ulcers by inhibiting growth of *Helicobacter*

pylori, the ulcer-causing bacterium. And all along you though garlic was only used to prepare pasta with tomato sauce and garlic bread.

When raw garlic is cut or smashed with a hard blow from the side of a French knife, an enzyme contained within the cell walls combines with the amino acids, creating a new compound called allicin, which has been shown to kill twenty-three types of bacteria, including salmonella and staphylococcus. After smashing or mincing the garlic, let it sit for fifteen minutes before cooking or consuming to allow the chemicals to activate. More affirmation that our Earth Suits are just big biochemical factories, which lends support to the theory that food is, indeed, good medicine.

But can too much of a good thing be bad? The answer: Besides the aesthetics, the only reported problem from eating ten or more cloves a day would be a minor irritation to the digestive tract, sometimes resulting in a case of flatulence. But who cares about that when the room is redolent of garlic? And if you're worried about the bad-breath issue, reach for that sprig of parsley on your plate. More than just a garnish, the chlorophyll it's loaded with is an outstanding breath freshener. (Remember Clorets chewing gum and how it touted chlorophyll as its active ingredient?)

FRESH IS ALWAYS THE BEST

Fresh garlic is far more effective than an over-the-counter supplement, and powdered or processed dry garlic is a waste of time, both from a culinary and health standpoint. Lose the garlic salt, granulated garlic, and garlic powder; they're all right for a spice rub, but that's about all. The processing and irradiation destroys the valuable nutrients.

California, the number one garlic producing state in the United States, grows over 500 million pounds of garlic a year on a mere 27,000 acres. Most of the 80 million pounds of garlic annually consumed in this country comes from California. History records

that missionaries introduced garlic, which is indigenous to south-west Siberia, to California.

If you plan on growing garlic yourself for your private stash, plant early in the spring, in March, and the bulbs should be ready for yanking in late August when the leaves begin to wither. However, if the summer is extraordinarily wet and cool, your garlic may probably not be ready until mid-September. Be patient.

According to *Modern Herbal, Herb Profile Information*, a garlic bed should be planted in sandy, loamy soil in a sunny area, must be kept thoroughly free from weeds, and the soil kept gathered up around the roots with occasional hoeing.

To this chef, when entering a kitchen, there is no sweeter elixir than that of the ethereal aroma of freshly minced raw garlic simmering over a low fire in a shimmering pool of golden, fruity olive oil. It's Pavlovian, as I respond with uncontrollable drooling and an increased appetite. My generous use of garlic is well documented by my friends and family, so it's no secret when I'm in the kitchen. My obsessive love for garlic has taught me, however, that it's always a good idea to serve a little food along with it.

You can never use too much garlic in my kitchen. Our favorite garlicky pasta dish, which I call "Sicilian Pasta," begins with first cooking one pound of your favorite whole-grain pasta al dente. Drain the pasta, but do not rinse it, and keep it warm. Next, add good quality olive oil to a skillet placed over medium heat, and to that add 2 tablespoons of freshly chopped garlic, 1 teaspoon or more of crushed red pepper flakes, several twists of freshly cracked pepper, and sea salt to taste. Simmer briefly for 1 minute, then add 1 can of tomato paste and 1 cup of vegetable stock and whisk into a smooth sauce. Finally, add the pasta and yet another 2—yes, 2!—tablespoons of chopped garlic and toss gently to coat. This dish should be topped with good Parmesan, Asiago cheese, or soy

Parmesan and garnished with strips of fresh basil. If it is too dry, add a bit more stock, as the warm pasta will continue to soak up moisture.

Between the garlic, the lycopene from the tomatoes, the hot pepper flakes, and the olive oil, this dish has tremendous health benefits. Mangia!

Raw garlic appears in multitudes of Mediterranean recipes. Provençal style includes the specialty *aioli*, a mayonnaise based on olive oil and enriched with garlic. The Greeks make *skordalia*, a paste made from cooked potatoes and raw garlic. And the Turks make a refreshing sauce called *cacik*, made from plain yogurt, shredded cucumber, garlic, and peppermint leaves.

A vampire doesn't have a chance in Vietnam where raw, grated garlic is served in liberal amounts in spring rolls and spicy noodle soups. Thai cooking avoids frying garlic; however, the Chinese fry it along with fresh ginger to create the aromatics of their dishes.

Remember, the longer you cook garlic the more pungency, strength, and odor is lost, and it becomes more subtle and less dominant. Garlic should harmonize with other herbs.

GARLIC TIPS

The basic rule of thumb when buying garlic is to choose firm, heavy, plump bulbs with dry skins; avoid soft or shriveled cloves, or those that have already sprouted. Unbroken bulbs can be stored six to eight weeks; individual cloves will keep three to ten days. The jarred version leaves much to be desired, so pass on it and make your own by using your food processor and good quality olive oil. Place the mix in a jar and store it in the refrigerator, but never at room temperature.

To roast garlic, rub the entire head in olive oil and wrap in aluminum foil, then place on a baking sheet into a 325-degree oven

until soft. Let cool until you're able to handle it, then squeeze the cloves from the skins.

Poaching unpeeled garlic cloves in milk will remove garlic's raw bitterness and heat. Use the garlic milk in a batch of mashed potatoes or to season a soup or casserole.

No self-respecting chef would be caught dead without fresh garlic in his or her larder. I strongly suggest that you follow suit and entertain your family's taste buds by enlisting fresh garlic as your first lieutenant in front-line defense of their most valuable and precious asset: their health. Eat it for your health as well as for your enjoyment. After all, what's a little stink among family and friends? One of the many valuable lessons I've learned along my road to wellness is that you can easily enjoy delicious foods and heal yourself and your loved ones, one loving spoonful at a time. A win-win situation for all.

The odiferous moral of this story: Loosen up a little and recognize that fresh garlic is at least a health food, and at most, good medicine. My motto: With a little stink, you can be in the pink!

Potent Pumpkin Power

O, it sets my hart a-clickin' like the tickin' of a clock,
When the frost is on the punkin and the fodder's in
the shock.

"When the Frost is on the Punkin"
James Whitcomb Riley (1849–1916)

I'm a sucker for nostalgia. When I think of pumpkins, my thoughts take me back in time to my childhood memories of autumn: gray, rainy days, the smoke from burning leaves hazing the air, hot cider, *outdoor* football games, snuggling during hay rides under harvest moons, and, of course, glowing jack-o'-lanterns.

Then there is the Thanksgiving memory of the aroma of a creamy, spicy pumpkin pie fresh from the oven accompanied by the perfume of a roasting turkey. *Speaking of pie: Is the ratio of a pumpkin's circumference to its diameter called "pumpkin pi"? The confusion comes from learning about "pi squared" in math class and Mom telling me that "pie are round"—an old southern Indiana joke.*

These are probably your pumpkin memories, too. But do you ever think of pumpkin as an everyday food that could improve your health?

It's true. Pumpkin is somewhat of a rising star on the nutritional block due to its high fiber, potassium, and vitamin content. According to research provided by Tufts University, pumpkin is a super cancer-fighting food. A mere one-half cup of pumpkin contains more than five times the standard RDA for beta carotene

(vitamin A) per day. Furthermore, beta carotene also provides protection against heart disease and many of the degenerative aspects of aging.

Now, let's think outside the gourd for a while. There you are, looking a whole pumpkin square in the eye, feeling unsure, and mumbling to yourself, "Now what do I do?"

Relax. It's not that big a deal. It's just a pumpkin. You can bake it, roast it, steam it, or throw it at Ichabod Crane. You can serve it cubed or mashed, and even make soup, bread, cake, and cookies with it. No matter how you prepare pumpkin, its potent power— the wonderful beta carotene, fiber, and vitamins—will add fresh ammo to your nutritional arsenal.

References to the versatile pumpkin date back about four centuries. According to the University of Illinois Extension, the name pumpkin originated from "pepon," the Greek word for "large melon." That word was nasalized by the French into "pompon," which was changed by the English to "pumpion." (Shakespeare referred to the "pumpion" in his *Merry Wives of Windsor*.) The American colonists changed "pumpion" into "pumpkin," and there we have it.

Pumpkins were a revered part of the Native American diet, and the pumpkin seeds were valued more for their oil and medicinal properties than the pumpkin flesh. The Mayans used the crushed seeds to treat kidney infections and intestinal parasites, and the juice was used to treat burns.

The golden globes quickly became a standby of the early New England settlements. In early Colonial times, settlers hollowed out large pumpkins, filled them with milk, eggs, honey or maple syrup, and cinnamon, and baked them in the hot ashes of their fireplaces. A Pilgrim verse from around 1633 said:

> For pottage, and pudding, and custards and pies
> Our pumpkins and parsnips are common supplies.
> We have pumpkins at morning and pumpkins at noon.
> If it were not for pumpkins, we should soon be undoon.

There are conflicting reports as to whether pumpkin was a part of the first Thanksgiving meals of the Pilgrims and the Indians. Regardless, since then, pumpkins have been and continue to be a wonderful tradition at the Thanksgiving Day table.

Other uses for pumpkins exist that only Peter, Peter, Pumpkin Eater and Cinderella could appreciate. Peter must have been out of his gourd to keep his wife locked up inside one, and Cinderella . . . well, as you recall, she tooled away from the ball in a four-wheel SUV version. So, as you can see, the pumpkin is quite versatile.

Our friends at the University of Illinois Extension offer a few potent pumpkin facts:

- Pumpkin seeds can be roasted as a nutritious zinc- and protein-loaded snack.
- Pumpkins contain potassium, vitamin A, C, and B.
- Pumpkins have more beta-carotene than any other produce.
- Pumpkins are used as feed for animals.
- Pumpkin flowers are edible.
- Pumpkins originated in Central America.
- The Connecticut field variety is the traditional American pumpkin.
- Pumpkins are 90 percent water.
- Pumpkins were once recommended for removing freckles and curing snake bites.
- Native Americans used pumpkin seeds for food and medicine.

Give Peas a Chance!

PUMPKIN NUTRITIONAL FACTS

(1 cup cooked, no salt)

Calories	49
Magnesium	22 mg
Potassium	564 mg
Zinc	1 mg
Selenium	.5 mg
Vitamin C	12 mg
Protein	2 grams
Carbohydrates	12 grams
Dietary fiber	3 grams
Calcium	37 mg
Iron	1.4 mg
Niacin	1 mg
Folate	21 mcg
Vitamin A	2650 IU
Vitamin E	3 mg

The conclusion you should be reaching is that pumpkin is very good for you. That is, until we begin adding ingredients that make up most pumpkin recipes: cream, butter, eggs, sugar, and shortening—especially shortening. (Do you know why they call it shortening? Because it shortens your life.)

Multitudes of pumpkin recipes are available. My favorite is to bake the meat of the pompion, mash it, add a little maple syrup, a pinch of salt, and a touch of cinnamon. Challenge yourself this autumn to add new and delicious pumpkin recipes to your year-round repertoire. Pumpkin soup, pumpkin bread, pumpkin pancakes, and pumpkin bars are just some of the many available recipes. Light and healthy versions can be found everywhere in the fall. And look through autumn issues of magazines such as *Vegetarian Times*, *Cooking Light*, and *Natural Health* for easy, family pleasing, healthy versions of your traditional favorites.

Tips for Healthy Eating

First and foremost, all the ingredients and produce you use in cooking should be certified organic.

WATER: filtered or spring water only

COOKING AND SALAD OILS: non-hydrogenated, expeller pressed, cold extracted. Instead of butter and shortening, I prefer trans-fat and cholesterol-free Smart Balance Buttery Spread

BAKING POWDER: non-aluminum

SEASONINGS: sea salt, kosher salt, Bragg Liquid Aminos, tamari or soy sauce

Flours: unbleached, whole grain preferred

SWEETENERS: Sucanat, stevia, brown rice syrup, real maple syrup, and xylitol crystals (*see below*).

WHAT TO AVOID: Artificial food colorings, caramel coloring, preservatives, phosphates, aluminum, bromaline, nitrates, nitrites, sulfites, and any other ingredient that does not come from nature's own laboratory

What is Xylitol

The new kid on the sweetener block, xylitol is a naturally occurring sweetener that is made from renewable resources. It is found in berries, mushrooms, lettuce, hard woods, and corncobs and is even produced by the human body itself.

- It's as sweet as suger, but with 40 percent fewer calories and 75 percent fewer carbohydrates

- It doesn't cause insulin reactions, making it ideal for diabetics and individuals who are hypoglycemic or on low-carb diets

- It's a 7 on the glycemic index (a ranking of the rise in serum glucose from different foods)

- It increases salivary flow, which reduces plaque formation on teeth, helps reduce the development of dental caries, and aids in the repair of damaged tooth enamel

- It may help prevent osteoporosis

- It impedes the development of strep bacteria in the mouth and intestines

❧

Healthy Conversions

Your body is not only your buddy, it is your temple, and you should show reverence by maintaining it well. As I've stressed in this book, your first line toward good health lies in what you eat. But after a lifetime of eating certain foods, change can be confusing. Let me clear away some of that confusion by offering tasty—and healthy—alternatives for traditional ingredients.

❧

Eggs

As a heart-attack survivor, I try to avoid eggs. But what is cooking without eggs? Try the following alternatives.

Egg Beaters®

¼ cup = 1 egg
2 tablespoons = 1 egg white
3 tablespoons = 1 egg yolk

Ener-G Egg Replacer®

One 16-ounce box equals 100 eggs. This is vegan-friendly—animal- and dairy-free. Look for it in whole foods stores.

HOMEMADE EGG SUBSTITUTES

For 1 egg, substitute one of the following:

2   tablespoons cornstarch
2   tablespoons arrowroot
2   tablespoons potato starch
1   heaping tablespoon soy powder + 2 tablespoons water
1   tablespoon soymilk powder + 1 tablespoon cornstarch + 2 tablespoons water
1   tablespoon ground flax seed + 1 cup water (grind the seeds in a coffee grinder, and blend with the water in a blender 1–2 minutes until desired consistency. This is also a great thickener for soups.)
1   banana (use for cakes)

LOW-CAL, LOW-CHOL EGG SUBSTITUTE

1   tablespoon nonfat dry milk
2   egg whites (from Grade A large organic eggs, of course!)
     Pinch of turmeric

Sprinkle the powdered milk over the egg whites and beat the dickens out of them with a fork or whisk until smooth. Add the turmeric and beat until blended. This equals ¼ cup, or 1 large egg. If you use this for scrambled eggs, cook in olive oil or Smart Balance so the "eggs" won't be too dry.

🐝

SWEETS FOR THE SWEETIES

Despite the fact that stevia has been used for centuries as a sweetener, the FDA has not approved it as such. So, look for it in the supplements section of your whole foods store. It's worth the hunt.

Keep in mind, though, that a little stevia goes a long way, so use these exchange guidelines:

Sugar amount	Stevia powder	Stevia liquid
1 cup	1 teaspoon	1 teaspoon
1 tablespoon	¼ teaspoon	6–9 drops
1 teaspoon	A pinch ($1/16$ teaspoon)	2–4 drops

🐝

"FLOUR" POWER

Many of us are sensitive to wheat gluten and dairy. Here's a terrific flour substitute:

6 cups rice flour
2 cups potato flour
1 cup tapioca flour

Combine all ingredients and store in an airtight container in a cool, dry area.

Appetizers, Snacks, and Beverages

Lord, Make me an instrument of Thy peace:
  Where there is hatred, let me sow love;
Where there is injury, pardon;
  Where there is doubt, faith;
Where there is despair, hope;
  Where there is darkness, light;
And where there is sadness, joy.

—Prayer of St. Francis of Assisi

Toasted Apple and Bleu Cheese Wrap with Walnuts and Wild Greens

1 cup water
2 tablespoons lemon juice
2 medium Granny Smith apples
1½ cups crumbled bleu cheese
3 tablespoons walnut pieces
3 cups greens, such as mesclun or field greens
6 tablespoons Smart Balance Buttery Spread
6 12-inch low-fat tortillas

In a small bowl, combine the water and lemon juice. Core the apples (don't peel 'em!), chop finely, and add to the water and lemon juice, stirring to coat. (This will keep the apples from oxidizing, or turning brown.) Drain the apples and pat dry, and combine with the bleu cheese, walnuts, and greens.

On one tortilla, place one-sixth of the apple mixture on the bottom third. Fold the sides of the tortilla toward the center, and roll up from the bottom. Repeat with the remaining tortillas and apple mixture.

Melt 2 tablespoons of the Smart Balance Buttery Spread in a large skillet over medium heat. Place two of the wraps in the skillet and cook, turning once, until golden brown. Repeat with the remaining wraps. Serves 6.

Salsaparagus

Who says salsa can be made only from tomatoes? This green dip explodes with flavor and wholesome nutrition.

1 pound asparagus, coarse stems removed, chopped small
1 small onion, finely chopped
1 teaspoon ground coriander
1 jalapeño pepper, seeded and minced
1 garlic clove, minced
2 tablespoons fresh lime juice
1 large tomato, finely diced and drained
1 cup tomato juice (if possible, use your juicer and make your own)
Sea salt and freshly cracked black pepper to taste

Have a large bowl of ice water standing by. Meanwhile, fill a stockpot one-third with water and bring to a boil. Toss in the asparagus, remove from heat, and let set for 2 minutes—no longer! Drain the asparagus and place in the ice water. (This will shock the green goody and help it retain its brilliant green color.)

After the asparagus has cooled, drain and combine with the remaining ingredients. Cover and chill for about 3 hours. Makes 4 cups.

Vegan Herbed White Bean Spread

1   15-ounce can cannellini beans, drained and rinsed
1   garlic clove, minced
1   tablespoon fresh lemon juice
        (or 1½ teaspoons vitamin C crystals)
1   teaspoon extra virgin olive oil
¼   teaspoon chopped fresh oregano
½   teaspoon ground cumin
     Sea salt and pepper to taste
¼   teaspooon cayenne

Combine all ingredients in the bowl of a food processor and process until smooth. Adjust seasonings to taste. If the mix is too stiff, add a little more lemon juice or olive oil. Transfer the mixture to a serving bowl, cover and refrigerate for a while for the flavors to marry.

To serve, allow the spread to come to room temperature, which will release the flavor. Garnish with more fresh oregano and a dusting of cayenne. Serves 4.

Baked American-Fried Potatoes

We love the French! But these are excellent substitutions for those animal-fat-laden, artery-clogging products of the deep fryer. (Actually, it was Thomas Jefferson who created the first "french fries.")

4	medium russet potatoes (leave the skins on)
2	tablespoons peanut oil
2	shallots, minced
2	cloves garlic, minced
	Cayenne pepper to taste
$1/4$	teaspoon each dried marjoram and thyme

Preheat oven to 450 degrees.

Cut the potatoes into $1/2$-inch strips and dry them thoroughly on paper toweling. In a large bowl, combine the oil, shallots, garlic, cayenne, marjoram, and thyme. Toss in the spuds and gently mix to coat.

Spread the potato strips evenly in a single layer on a large sheet pan, leaving a smidge of space between the strips so all sides can cook evenly. Bake for 15 minutes, turning with a spatula a few times, until the potatoes are tender and a crispy golden brown. Serves 4.

Indian Potato Patties

2	large russet potatoes, finely diced
1/4	cup diced onion
1/4	cup chopped cashew pieces
1/4	cup freshly chopped parsley
1/2	chopped red bell pepper
1/2	chopped green bell pepper
1/4	cup diced tomatoes, with their juice
1	teaspoon fresh chopped ginger
1	teaspoon sea salt
1/4	cup whole wheat flour
	Vegetable oil

Combine all ingredients except the oil. Shape into patties and refrigerate for at least an hour.

Add just enough oil to a large skillet to cover the bottom and heat over medium heat. Fry the patties until golden brown on one side. (Avoid crowding them.) Turn the patties and cook until the other side is also golden brown. Drain on paper towels and serve. Makes 16 patties.

Note: If you are gluten sensitive, substitute amaranth, kamut, or spelt flour for the whole wheat flour.

Mock Crab Cakes

7	slices whole wheat bread, broken into large pieces
1/4	cup olive oil
3/4	cup finely diced celery
3/4	cup finely chopped white onion
1/2	cup minced carrot
1	small green bell pepper, minced
1	tablespoon dried tarragon
1/4	cup chopped parsley
16	ounces firm tofu, pressed and drained
2	tablespoons sherry
4	drops Tabasco sauce
3/4	cup mayonnaise
1	teaspoon sea salt and cracked black pepper to taste
2	tablespoons Old Bay seasoning

Preheat oven to 350 degrees.

In a food processor or blender, process bread pieces into fine crumbs. Place on a baking sheet and bake for 8–10 minutes, or until dried and toasty. Remove from oven and set aside.

In a skillet, warm the olive oil over medium-high heat and sauté the celery, onion, carrot, and pepper until tender, about 5 minutes. Remove from heat and stir in the tarragon and parsley.

In a food processor, pulse the tofu just to a cottage cheese-type consistency. In a large bowl, combine it with the sherry and Tabasco. Add the sautéed vegetables, 1/2 cup of the breadcrumbs, the mayonnaise, and seasonings. Mix well.

Shape the mixture into patties about 3 inches in diameter and 1/2-inch thick. Dredge the patties with the remaining breadcrumbs and arrange on a baking sheet sprayed with vegetable spray. Lightly spray the tops of the patties. Bake 15 minutes, flip, and bake about 10 minutes longer, or until golden. Makes 10 cakes.

Pinto Bean and Toasted Corn Salsa

1	15-ounce can pinto beans, drained and rinsed
1	10-ounce bag frozen corn, thawed (or the equivalent of fresh)
1	large tomato, diced (or 1 can diced tomatoes)
2	tablespoons fresh cilantro
1	cup diced onion
1	red bell pepper, finely diced
2	teaspoons minced garlic
2	teaspoons ground cumin
1	tablespoon honey
1	tablespoon chili powder
3	teaspoons lime juice
3	tablespoons extra virgin olive oil
	Sea salt and cracked black pepper to taste

This one's a real toughie! Dump everything into a large bowl, mix, cover, and set in the fridge. Then chill out. This combo gets a whole lot better after the flavors marry and honeymoon for a while. Serves 6–8.

Basic Granola

*Granola's not just for breakfast. Eat it anytime you need a
pick-me-up. And it's a great take-along snack.*

5	pounds rolled quick-cooking oats
1	pound chopped walnuts
1	pound toasted, unsalted sunflower seeds
1	cup toasted, unsalted pumpkin seeds
1	cup honey
2	tablespoons vanilla extract
2	tablespoons ground cinnamon
1	teaspoon sea salt
1	cup raisins
1	cup dried cranberries or raisins

Preheat oven to 325 degrees.

In a large mixing bowl, combine the oats, walnuts, sunflower seeds,
and pumpkin seeds.

In a saucepan, combine the honey, vanilla extract, cinnamon, and
salt. Whisk to blend and heat over low heat just until warm. Pour the
honey mixture over the oats mixture. Using your fingers like rakes,
stir the mixture up from the bottom until the oats mixture is evenly
coated. (Wear plastic food service gloves for this process—it's
messy.)

Working in batches, spread the mixture on a large sheet pan in about
a ¼-inch layer. Bake 20–25 minutes, stirring frequently, until the
mixture is toasted to your preference. Let cool, add the dry fruit, and
mix. Store in airtight bags or containers.

Note: Make a big batch of this—it freezes beautifully.

Granola Bars

*These homemade granola bars are so easy to make, and
tasty too. I like chopped walnuts and dried cranberries in
mine, but any dried fruit and nuts will be just as good.
These make terrific snacks to pack in the kids' lunches.*

3	cups rolled oats
1	cup coarsely chopped nuts
1	cup raw, unsalted sunflower seeds
1	cup dried fruit
1	teaspooon cinnamon
1	can sweetened condensed milk
1/8	teaspooon vanilla extract
1/2	cup melted butter or Smart Balance Buttery Spread

Preheat oven to 325 degrees.

Combine the oats, nuts, sunflower seeds, fruit, and cinnamon in a
large bowl. Combine the sweetened condensed milk, vanilla extract,
and butter or Smart Balance Buttery Spread, and add to the oats
mixture. Stir until well blended.

Line a 10-by-15-inch sheet pan with foil and spray the foil with
vegetable cooking spray. Spoon the granola mixture into the pan, and
pat it gently down with your hands. (To keep the mixture from
sticking to your hands, dampen them first.) Bake 25–30 minutes or
until golden brown. Let cool slightly, remove from pan, and peel off
the foil. Finish cooling and cut into bars.

Note: If you want to cut the fat, replace the butter with 1/2 cup of
applesauce.

Mayan Chocolate

5   cups low-fat milk, or plain soy or rice milk
    Honey to taste
1   cinnamon stick
$1/8$ teaspoon cayenne pepper
$1/8$ teaspoon nutmeg
3   ounces unsweetened chocolate, or $1/3$ cup good-quality cocoa
      powder
1   ounce milk chocolate

Combine the milk, honey, cinnamon stick, cayenne, and nutmeg in a large saucepan. Stirring constantly, heat the milk over medium-low heat just until hot, but not boiling.

Melt the chocolate a smidge in the microwave and add it to the hot milk mixture. If using cocoa powder, incorporate it with a whisk. Add the honey.

Remove the cinnamon stick. With a hand mixer, whip the mixture until frothy, pour into cups, and serve. Serves 4.

Mango Iced Tea

1   26-ounce jar mango slices
2   tea bags
      Sweetener of choice (such as stevia or honey) to taste
      Juice of one lime

Drain the mangoes and reserve the syrup. Add enough water to the syrup to make 4 cups and pour into a large nonreactive saucepan. Over medium-high heat, bring the liquid just to a boil. Remove from heat, add the teabags, and let steep for 5 minutes. (No longer than that or the mixture will become bitter.)

In a blender or food processor, puree the mangos. Strain the pureed mangoes through a sieve and add to the syrup and tea mixture. Add the sweetener and lime juice and mix well. Garnish with lime wedges or slices. Serves 6–8.

Soups, Salads, and Sauces

If there is light in the soul,
    There will be beauty in the person.
If there is beauty in the person,
    There will be harmony in the house.
If there is harmony in the house,
    There will be order in the nation.
If there is order in the nation,
    There will be peace in the world.

—Chinese Proverb

Basic Vegetable Stock

This easy-to-make stock can replace chicken or beef stocks when making soups, stews, and sauces. And it freezes beautifully.

8   cups water
1   cup dry white wine
1   14.5-ounce can diced tomatoes, with juice
1   bay leaf
1   teaspoon each dried thyme, basil, and oregano
2   tablespoons extra virgin olive oil
1   cup stemmed, thinly sliced shiitakes
1   apple, unpeeled, cored and diced
2   medium potatoes, unpeeled, cubed
2   medium carrots, unpeeled, diced
2   stalks celery, diced
1   large onion, diced
3   cloves garlic (or more, if you like), slightly smashed
1   red bell pepper, diced
1   green bell pepper, diced

In a large stockpot, combine the water, wine, tomatoes, bay leaf, and herbs. Bring to a boil, then reduce heat and simmer for 1 hour. Remove the bay leaf and return the stock to the pot.

In a large skillet, heat the olive oil over medium-high heat and sauté the mushrooms, apple, and vegetables just until slightly tender. Add the vegetables to the stock, bring just to a boil, then reduce heat and simmer for 45 minutes. Strain out the vegetables. If you like, reserve them to use later in a soup, or you can puree them and return them to the stock for a thicker consistency. Makes about 2 quarts.

Corn Chowder

1   cup nonfat dry milk
4   tablespoons cornstarch
3   cups soymilk
1   cup chopped celery
1   large onion, chopped
4   cups of vegetable stock or water
4   cups diced potatoes
4   cups frozen corn
$^1/_2$ teaspoon each of dried marjoram, thyme, oregano, basil, and
      rosemary
1   drop liquid smoke
    Sea salt to taste
    Chopped fresh parsley

In a small bowl, thoroughly whisk the dry milk and cornstarch into the plain soymilk.

Place the celery and onion into a large soup pot and add the stock or water. Bring to a boil, then reduce heat to medium-low and simmer until vegetables are tender, about 10 minutes. Add the remaining ingredients except the soymilk mixture. Cover and continue cooking over medium heat until the potatoes are tender, about 20 minutes.

Remove about 2 cups of the chowder and place in a blender or food processor. Puree and return to the soup pot. Add the soymilk mixture and salt to taste, stir well and heat thoroughly. If the chowder seems too thick, adjust by adding more liquid, a bit at a time, until desired consistency. Garnish with parsley and serve. Serves 8.

Quinoa Corn Chowder

2	cups water
¼	cup quinoa, thoroughly rinsed
2	cups diced new red potatoes
¼	cup diced carrot
¼	cup chopped onion
2	cups corn
2	cups low-fat milk, or plain soymilk
1	teaspoon sea salt
	Dash of black pepper
¼	cup chopped parsley
	Butter, olive oil, or Smart Balance Buttery Spread

In a large pot, combine the water, quinoa, potatoes, carrot, and onion. Bring to a boil, then reduce heat and simmer until the vegetables are tender, about 15 minutes. Add the corn, increase heat just until the soup begins to boil again, then again reduce heat and simmer another 15 minutes. Add the milk and seasonings, and bring just to a boil one last time, then remove from heat. Garnish with parsley and a conservative blob of butter, olive oil, or Smart Balance Buttery Spread—it's your call. Serves 4–6.

Adapted from a recipe from Quinoa Corporation,
Ancient Harvest, Gardena, California

Quinoa Vegetable Soup

4 cups cooked quinoa
1 tablespoon safflower oil
½ cup diced carrots
½ cup diced celery
2 tablespoons chopped onions
¼ cup chopped green pepper
2 cloves garlic, chopped
4 cups water
½ cup diced tomatoes
½ cup chopped cabbage
1 teaspoon sea salt
Chopped parsley

In a stockpot, heat oil and add the quinoa, carrots, celery, onions, green pepper, and garlic, and sauté until lightly browned. Add the water, tomatoes, and cabbage, and bring just to a boil. Reduce heat and simmer for 20–30 minutes or until vegetables are tender. Season to taste and garnish with parsley. Serves 4–6.

Adapted from a recipe from Quinoa Corporation,
Ancient Harvest, Gardena, California

Tuscan Bean Soup

A savory potage I like to call "a no-brainer."

2   15-ounce cans white beans (cannellini preferred)
3   cups vegetable stock
1   clove garlic, minced
1   medium onion, chopped
1   carrot, chopped
1   stalk celery, chopped
2   leeks, white and tender green parts only, chopped
1   sprig fresh rosemary, leaves only, chopped
1   green bell pepper, chopped
3   drops of liquid smoke
    Sea salt and freshly cracked black pepper to taste
    Grated Parmesan cheese or tofu Parmesan
    Thinly sliced red onion rings

Rinse and drain the beans and place in large soup pot. Add the stock and the remaining ingredients and gently simmer for 15 minutes or until the vegetables are tender. Stir frequently.

(If you wish, sauté the vegetables in 2 tablespoons of olive oil and then add to the beans. If you decide to put it all together at once, you have my permission to still add the oil or leave it out altogether to turn this into a very low-fat meal.)

Garnish with grated Parmesan cheese and the red onion. Serve accompanied by a lusty, heavy, whole grain bread and a glass of dry red wine, if you wish. Serves 4.

Mexican "Meatball" Soup

3	tablespoons olive oil
1	medium onion, chopped
2	cloves garlic, minced
1	fresh jalapeño pepper, minced
1/2	teaspoon chili powder
1/4	teaspoon ground cumin
1/2	teaspoon cinnamon
2	quarts vegetable stock
1 1/2	cups chopped tomatoes
1/4	cup cooked brown rice
1	pound prepared seitan or "fake" wheat meat, cut into bite-size pieces
1	teaspoon sea salt
1/2	teaspoon freshly cracked black pepper
	Fresh cilantro, nonfat sour cream, and grated cheddar or soy cheese

Heat the olive oil in a stockpot over medium heat, and sauté the onion, garlic, and jalapeño pepper until translucent. Add the chili powder, cumin, and cinnamon and sauté a bit longer, stirring frequently to prevent scorching.

Deglaze the pan with the stock, add tomatoes and rice, and bring to a rapid boil. Reduce heat to medium and add the seitan or meat substitute and seasonings and cook, covered, over medium heat for 15 minutes, stirring frequently.

Ladle the soup into pre-warmed bowls and garnish with cilantro, sour cream, and cheese as desired. Serve with low-fat tortilla chips or toasted whole grain bread. Serves 6.

Sizzling Tex-Mex Tempeh Stew

Serve this forcefully flavored, fiery fricassee over a bed of whole grains or whole grain pasta, and garnish with chopped cilantro and green onions. Ice-cold beer is a must.

1	8-ounce package of tempeh
2	tablespoons olive oil
1½	teaspoons ground cumin
¾	teaspoon chili powder
1	medium onion, finely chopped
½	cup sliced mushrooms (your choice)
1	cup corn
1	red bell pepper, finely diced
2	small chipotle peppers in adobo, finely minced (reserve the adobo sauce)
1	tablespoon soy sauce
3	squares unsweetened chocolate
½	teaspoon instant espresso powder
1	4-ounce can chopped green chiles, with juice
1	14-ounce can diced tomatoes
1	can strong beer (optional)
	Sea salt and cracked pepper to taste
	Chopped cilantro and diced scallions
	Grated cheddar or soy cheddar cheese

Cut the tempeh into ½-inch cubes. Over medium heat, sauté the tempeh in 1 tablespoon of olive oil about 20 minutes or until lightly browned, breaking it up with the back of your spoon to crumble it. Add the cumin, chili powder, mushrooms, corn, and red bell pepper and sauté for about 5 minutes.

Combine the minced chipotle pepper, soy sauce, chocolate, espresso, green chiles, tomatoes, beer, and salt and pepper.

Simmer for another 10–20 minutes. If it gets too dry, add a smidge more beer, but cook it long enough to cook out the alcohol. If you like, drain some of the beer down your throat, but remember, "Too many cooks spoil the broth, but too much broth can spoil the cook!"

Serve garnished with the chopped cilantro and scallions and grated cheese. Serves 4–6.

"New" Old-Fashioned Bean Salad

1/2   cup vegetable or peanut oil
1/2   cup rice wine vinegar
1/2   teaspoon sea salt
1   teaspoon coriander
1/2   teaspoon black pepper
3/4   cup Sucanat or 1 tablespoon stevia powder
1   cup shelled fresh edamame beans
1   15-ounce can kidney beans, drained and rinsed
1   15-ounce can yellow wax beans, drained and rinsed
1   15-ounce can French-cut green beans, drained and rinsed
1/2   cup each diced red and green bell pepper
1   medium red onion, thinly sliced
2   tablespoons chopped fresh parsley

Combine the oil, vinegar, salt, coriander, pepper, and Sucanat or stevia. Blend well and refrigerate, covered, at least 2 hours. (Overnight is even better.)

Steam the edamame for 5 minutes. Let cool.

Combine the edamame with the other beans, and peppers, onion, and parsley.

Pour on the oil and vinegar mixture, gently toss, and refrigerate until serving time. Gravity happens, so toss the salad again before serving to distribute the flavorful dressing pooled at the bottom of the bowl. Serves 6–8.

Warm Green Bean and Mushroom Salad

*Shiitakes are renowned for their ability to
stimulate the immune system.*

1   pound fresh green beans, cleaned and trimmed
1   pound shiitake mushrooms, stemmed, and thinly sliced
2   tablespoons olive oil
2   tablespoons vegetable stock
2   tablespoons balsamic vinegar
1   red bell pepper, seeded and diced
1   yellow bell pepper, seeded and diced
$1/8$ teaspoon sea salt
     Fresh ground black pepper to taste

In a large pot with a steamer basket, bring water to a boil. Add the green beans and steam for 5–7 minutes. Drain and set aside.

Lightly spray a skillet with vegetable cooking spray, and sauté the mushrooms over medium heat until they give up their liquid. Meanwhile, in a large bowl, combine the oil, stock, and vinegar, and whisk to blend. Add the mushrooms, green beans, and bell peppers. Season with salt and pepper and toss to coat well. Serves 4.

Brown Rice Salad with "Meat"

*Throughout the Mediterranean, chilled rice salads
routinely appear on the family dinner table and are a
substantially filling but not heavy dish and a wonderful
base for fresh garden vegetables. Rather than mayonnaise, I prefer an olive oil and vinegar or lemon dressing
since I don't have to worry about it spoiling—besides,
it's healthier. I've found that long-grain brown basmati
rice is best for cold rice salads since it has less gluten
and holds its texture longer without breaking down.*

1	cup long-grain brown rice, basmati preferred
2½	cups water
1	teaspoon sea salt
⅔	cup extra-virgin olive oil
2	tablespoons red wine vinegar
¼	cup fresh lemon juice
1	tablespoon Dijon mustard
½	cup chopped fennel bulb or celery
½	cup finely diced red onion
¼	cup chopped fresh parsley
1	tablespoon chopped fresh tarragon
4	tablespoons olive oil
4	garlic cloves, finely minced
¼	teaspoon crushed red pepper flakes
1	teaspoon paprika
1	pound beef- or chicken-flavored meat substitute, cut in bite-size pieces
	Tomato wedges and avocado slices

Preheat oven to 400 degrees. In a lidded baking dish, combine the
rice, water, and salt. Cover and bake for 45 minutes. Remove from

oven and let stand, covered, for about 10 minutes or until the liquid is absorbed.

In a small bowl, make a vinaigrette by whisking together the $^2/_3$ cup olive oil, vinegar, lemon juice, and Dijon mustard. Adjust flavor with sea salt and pepper to taste. Transfer the warm rice to a bowl and drizzle with some of the vinaigrette, toss well, and let cool. Add the fennel or celery, onion, parsley, and tarragon, and toss again.

In a sauté pan, over medium heat, warm the 4 tablespoons of olive oil. Add the garlic, crushed red pepper flakes, and paprika, and cook for 1 minute. Increase heat to medium-high, add the meat substitute, and sauté for about 3 minutes, or until the meat substitute begins to brown. Season with salt and pepper to taste, remove from heat, and let set until cooled.

To serve, spoon a mound of the rice onto serving plates, top with the meat substitute, and drizzle with the remaining vinaigrette. (Or you can arrange the salad on a large platter and serve family-style.) Garnish with fresh tomato wedges and avocado slices, if desired. Serves 4.

Oven-Roasted Potato Salad

2½   pounds new red or Yukon Gold potatoes, peels on
      Extra virgin olive oil
      Sea salt and fresh cracked black pepper to taste
½   cup rice vinegar
 3   tablespoons olive oil
¼   cup chopped fresh parsley
¼   cup chopped fresh basil leaves
 4   green onions, thinly sliced
 1   cup diced fresh tomatoes (fresh is a must)
 1   cup corn, fresh or frozen (thawed)

Preheat oven to 425 degrees.

Quarter the potatoes. In a large mixing bowl, toss the potatoes with just enough olive oil to lightly coat and add the salt and pepper.

Spread the potatoes on a sheet pan and roast for about 45 minutes, or just until fork-tender and golden. Place the potatoes in a large bowl and add the rice vinegar, 3 tablespoons of olive oil, parsley, basil, green onions, tomatoes, and corn. Gently mix using a wooden or soft plastic spoon to avoid breaking up the potatoes. Adjust seasonings as desired. Serve at room temperature. Serves 6 as a side dish, or 3 as an entree.

Summer Potato and Radish Salad

This is a refreshing alternative to the predictably ordinary potato salad.

1¼   pounds new red or Yukon Gold potatoes, unpeeled
1   medium cucumber, thinly sliced
2   teaspoons sea salt
2   tablespoons Dijon mustard
2   tablespoons extra virgin olive oil
1   tablespoon rice wine vinegar
¼   cup assorted fresh herbs of your choice, chopped
1   bunch radishes, thinly sliced

In a large pan, boil the potatoes for 20 minutes or until tender. Do not overcook.

Meanwhile, sprinkle the cucumbers with salt, toss lightly, and set aside for 20 minutes to draw out the excess water.

In a small bowl, whisk together the mustard, olive oil, vinegar, and herbs. When the potatoes are cool enough to handle, cut into bite-size pieces. Gently toss with the mustard and oil mixture to coat.

Drain the excess liquid from the cucumbers. Arrange the cucumber slices around the edges of a serving platter and arrange the radish slices inside the cucumber edging. Mound the potatoes in the middle of the platter and serve. Serves 4.

Crunchy Cabbage and Onion Slaw

FOR THE DRESSING:
- 1/4 cup reduced-fat ricotta cheese
- 1/4 cup plain nonfat yogurt
- 3 tablespoons finely grated onion
- 2 1/2 tablespoons rice wine vinegar
- 1 clove garlic, minced
- 2 teaspoons Dijon mustard
- 2 tablespoons honey (or 1 teaspoon stevia or 2 teaspoons Splenda)
- 1 teaspoon celery salt
- 1 teaspoon celery seed
  Sea salt and pepper to taste

Combine all ingredients in a blender or food processor and process until smooth and creamy.

FOR THE SALAD:
- 1/2 cup chopped parsley
- 1 medium carrot, grated
- 2 cups shredded cabbage
- 1 medium onion, sliced super thin
- 1 bunch green onions, chopped

In a large bowl, combine the salad ingredients. Add the dressing and toss the dickens out of it. Serves 8.

Note: Try this slaw as a sandwich topping and watch your family flip out at the flavor!

Dutch Cole Slaw

$^1/_2$ cup tarragon vinegar
 2   tablespoons honey, or 1 tablespoon stevia powder
$^1/_8$ teaspoon celery seed
     Sea salt and black pepper to taste
$^1/_2$ medium head cabbage, finely chopped
 1   green bell pepper, finely chopped
 1   medium onion, finely chopped
 1   medium cucumber, finely chopped
 3   fresh tomatoes, diced
     Sea salt to taste

In a large mixing bowl, whisk together the vinegar, sweetener, celery seed, and salt and pepper. Blend well.

Add the cabbage and remaining ingredients and blend well, mixing up from the bottom to incorporate the dressing. Cover and refrigerate for 1 hour, stirring at least one more time before serving. Serves 4.

Dorothy's Sauerkraut Salad

*My friend Dorothy gave me this old family recipe using
tangy sauerkraut, an excellent tonic for the GI tract.*

½	cup extra virgin olive oil
¼	cup water
¾	cup Sucanat (or sweeten to taste with another sugar substitute, such as stevia)
½	cup rice wine vinegar
1	20-ounce can sauerkraut, well drained
1	green or red bell pepper, diced
1	medium onion, chopped
1	cup chopped celery
1	small jar pimentos, drained and chopped

Combine the olive oil, water, sweetener, and rice vinegar. Mix well and refrigerate, covered, overnight. (NOTE: This dressing will keep beautifully for at least a week.)

In a large bowl, combine the sauerkraut, bell pepper, onion, celery, and pimento. Add the dressing and toss to mix. Serves 4.

"Sneaky" Chicken Salad

Prepare this savory recipe several hours ahead of serving time to allow the flavors to marry. Your patience will be rewarded.

1 8-ounce package tempeh, cut into $\frac{1}{2}$-inch pieces
$\frac{1}{2}$ cup each diced red and green bell pepper
$\frac{1}{2}$ cup chopped celery
$\frac{1}{2}$ cup diced red onion
1 teaspoon Dijon mustard
2 tablespoons sweet pickle relish
2 tablespoon wheat germ or ground flax seed
   Sea salt and black pepper to taste
$\frac{1}{8}$ teaspoon poultry seasoning
$\frac{1}{2}$ teaspoon turmeric
1 teaspoon chopped parsley
$\frac{1}{2}$ cup Vegetarian Mayonnaise (page 152)

Steam the tempeh for 15 minutes. Let it cool and combine with the remaining ingredients. Mix well until the tempeh breaks up a bit. Serve on bread as sandwiches, or on a bed of wild greens garnished with fresh tomato wedges and olives. Serves 4–6.

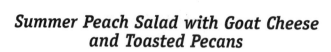

Summer Peach Salad with Goat Cheese and Toasted Pecans

 1   cup pecan halves
 1/2 cup balsamic vinegar
 1   bay leaf
 1/4 cup walnut oil
 2   teaspoons honey
 1   6-ounce log goat cheese
 1/4 cup whole wheat bread crumbs
 2   peaches, unpeeled, cut into 1-inch pieces
 5   cups mixed baby greens
     Fresh cracked black

Spread the pecan halves on a baking sheet and toast in the oven at 375 degrees for about 5 minutes. As soon as you notice the lovely, nutty aroma, they're done. Remove from oven and let cool, then coarsely chop and set aside.

In a small saucepan, bring the balsamic vinegar to a boil. Add the bay leaf, reduce the heat to low, and simmer until the balsamic vinegar reduces to about 1/8 cup. Remove from the heat and add the walnut oil and honey. Discard the bay leaf and let the mixture cool.

Preheat oven to 400 degrees. Slice the goat cheese into 6 equal pieces and coat with the breadcrumbs. Place the goat cheese slices on a sheet pan and bake 6–7 minutes, or until the cheese is soft and the crumbs are golden.

Toss the greens together with the peaches and balsamic vinegar dressing. Arrange on chilled salad plates, sprinkle with the toasted pecans, and top with the delicate, beautiful goat cheese. Sprinkle with cracked black pepper as desired and serve. Serves 6.

Warm Apple Cider Dressing

2   cups unfiltered apple cider
3   tablespoons apple cider vinegar
2   teaspoons prepared brown mustard
2   tablespoons olive oil
    Sea salt and fresh cracked black pepper to taste

Over high heat, bring the cider to a boil in a nonreactive saucepan. Boil for 15 minutes, or until the cider reduces by half, scraping down the sides of the pan occasionally as it cooks. Whisk in the vinegar, mustard, olive oil, and black pepper. Adjust the seasonings to taste. Keep covered in the refrigerator. Makes about $1^1/_2$ cups.

Flax Seed Vinaigrette

Flax seed is a wonderful source of the essential fatty acids that are so good for your heart's health!

$^1/_2$ cup cold-pressed flaxseed oil
3   tablespoons lemon juice or rice vinegar
3   tablespoons water
1   teaspoon tamari
3   cloves garlic, minced
$^1/_2$ teaspoon maple syrup or honey
1   teaspoon Dijon mustard
2   tablespoons fresh chopped tarragon or oregano

Combine all ingredients in a blender and puree until smooth. Cover and store in the refrigerator. This will keep for up to 5 days. Makes about 1 cup.

Creamy Miso Dressing

Miso—fermented soybean paste—is an essential weapon in your healthy arsenal. Some may equate "fermented" with "spoiled," but that's not the case. Miso and other fermented food products, including sauerkraut, pickles, sourdough breads, tempeh, and yogurt, are great colon toners, helping to maintain the balance between beneficial microbes and those that are harmful. "Probiotic" supplements found in whole foods markets are just fine.

¹/₃	cup rice wine vinegar
4	tablespoons white miso
3	cloves garlic, crushed
2	tablespoons honey
2	teaspoons minced fresh ginger
¹/₂	cup peanut or vegetable oil
	Sea salt and black pepper to taste

Combine all ingredients except the oil in a blender and puree. With the blender running, add the oil in a slow, steady stream, and process until the mixture emulsifies. Add salt and pepper. Serve as a salad dressing or on sandwiches or pasta, or as a dip for vegetables. Makes about 1 cup.

Guacamole Salad Dressing

2   ripe avocados, peeled and pitted
1   medium onion, finely chopped
1   jalapeño pepper, seeded and finely chopped
    Juice of 1 lime
1   teaspoon sea salt
1   medium tomato, finely chopped
½   teaspoon cracked black pepper
3   tablespoons plain yogurt

Combine all ingredients in a blender or food processor, and puree until creamy. Cover and chill. Stir gently before serving. Makes about 2 cups.

Lime Marinade

This tart dressing is an excellent marinade for tofu and tempeh. It also doubles as a delightful salad dressing and is a good source of vitamin C.

¼   cup lime juice
2   tablespoons sherry
2   shallots, minced
1   tablespoon honey or stevia powder
1   teaspoon minced fresh ginger
2   tablespoons vegetable oil
1   teaspoon vitamin C crystals
1   teaspoon ground fennel seed
    Cayenne pepper, black pepper, and sea salt to taste

Combine all ingredients in a jar and shake well to blend. Keep chilled. Makes 1 cup.

Sweet and Sour Dressing

Use this hearty, all-purpose sauce for egg rolls,
stir-fry, veggies, pasta, salad dressing, or as a
glaze for tempeh or tofu.

1	pineapple, peeled, cored, and cubed
¼	cup peanut or soybean oil
2	tablespoons chopped fresh garlic
¼	cup finely minced fresh ginger
2	cups rice wine vinegar
1	cup vegetable stock
2	tablespoons tomato paste
1	can diced green chiles
2	tablespoons chile-garlic paste
	Sea salt to taste
2	tablespoons Sucanat (or 1 tablespoon stevia or 1 tablespoon honey)
3	tablespoons cornstarch
3	tablespoons water

In a food processor or blender, puree the pineapple.

In small saucepan combine the oil, ginger, and garlic, and sauté over medium heat for about 1 minute to release the aromatic flavors into the oil. Add the vinegar, vegetable stock, tomato paste, chiles, chile-garlic paste, salt, and sweetener, and whisk to incorporate. Add the pureed pineapple, including the juice. Simmer on medium-low heat for 5 minutes, stirring frequently.

Strain the mixture through a sieve. Return it to the saucepan and the heat.

Combine the cornstarch and water and stir to make a slurry. Bring the sauce to a boil and add the slurry a bit at a time until the sauce thickens. It should not be too thick, but if that happens, you can thin it out with a little fruit juice.

Store, covered, in the refrigerator. This will keep for 3 days. Makes about 4 cups.

Berry Ketchup

*This beautiful sauce can be used as a salad dressing
or as a marinade. As a dressing, it's wonderful
garnished with toasted slivered almonds.*

1/4	cup olive oil
2	teaspoons honey mustard
2	teaspoons raspberry vinegar
	Sea salt and fresh cracked pepper to taste
1	clove garlic, finely minced
1	tablespoon finely chopped fresh basil (or 1 teaspoon dried)
2	teaspoons Sucanat, or 1 teaspoon stevia powder
1/2	pint fresh raspberries
1/2	pint fresh blueberries

In a blender or food processor, puree the berries. (I like to keep the berry seeds and skins because they're loaded with nutrition, as well as beneficial Omega 3 fatty acids. But if you prefer otherwise, strain the pureed berries through a sieve to remove the seeds and skins.)

In a bowl whisk together the berry puree and remaining ingredients. Store refrigerated. Makes about 1½ cups.

Vegetarian Mayonnaise

*Hold the mayo! Traditional mayonnaise, with its egg yolks,
is bad for our hearts and adds to our "love handles." This
is a fantastic alternative.*

3	tablespoons lemon juice
1/2	cup plain soymilk
1/4	teaspoon sea salt
1/4	teaspoon paprika
1/4	teaspoon prepared mustard
6	tablespoons vegetable oil

Put all the ingredients except the oil into a blender and process on the lowest speed. As the blender runs, add the oil in a slow, continuous stream. Continue blending until thickened and smooth. Store covered in the refrigerator. Makes about 3/4 cup.

Mustard Dressing

3	tablespooons water
2	tablespooons tahini
1	tablespooon balsamic vinegar
1 1/2	teaspoons Dijon mustard
1	1-inch piece fresh ginger, peeled and minced
1/2	teaspoon minced garlic
1	teaspoon chopped parsley
1/2	cup extra virgin olive oil

In a blender or food processor, combine all ingredients except the oil and process until smooth. With the blender or food processor running, very slowly, in a steady stream, add the olive oil and process until the sauce emulsifies. (Emulsification prevents the dressing from separating.) Makes about 1 cup.

Beans, Grains, and Pasta

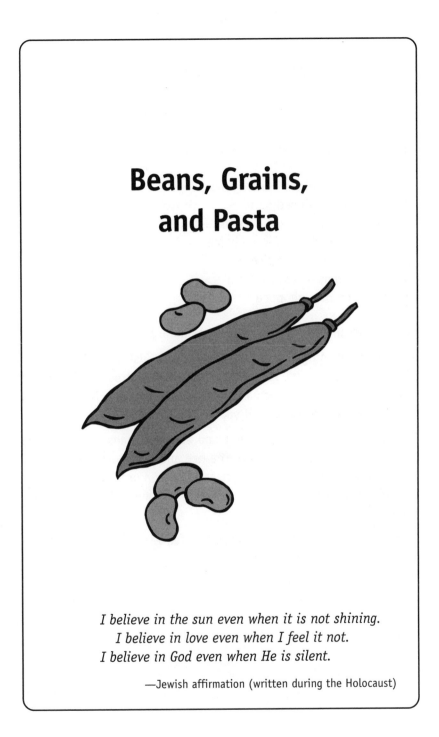

I believe in the sun even when it is not shining.
I believe in love even when I feel it not.
I believe in God even when He is silent.

—Jewish affirmation (written during the Holocaust)

Beans and Rice Asian-Style

This freezes well, and it makes great single suppers.

1   tablespoon toasted sesame oil
1   carrot, diced
1   tablespoon minced fresh ginger
1   tablespoon minced garlic
    Crushed red pepper flakes to taste (optional)
2   cup cooked beans (your choice)
3   cups cooked brown rice
3   tablespoons low sodium soy sauce
3   green onions, chopped

Heat the sesame oil in a skillet over medium heat.

Add the carrot, ginger, and garlic and stir-fry just until the carrot is slightly tender. Do not to overcook or you'll destroy the beneficial nutrients in the carrot, such as the beta carotene. Now is the time to add the crushed red pepper, if you're using it.

Turn up the heat to medium-hot and add the beans, rice, and soy sauce. Continue stir-frying until the rice and beans are suitably hot. Remove the pan from the heat, stir in the green onions, and serve. If you like, top with toasted sesame seeds or chopped fresh cilantro. Serves 4–6.

Note: Peas make a delightful substitute for beans. Just toss them in at the last minute before serving.

Southern Black-Eyed Peas

This recipe is an exercise in simplicity.

1   pound dry black-eyed peas
2   quarts water
1   onion, chopped
¼   cup green bell pepper, chopped
1   stalk celery, chopped
2   drops liquid smoke (or to taste)
1   8-ounce package seitan ("wheat meat") (optional)
    Sea salt and fresh cracked black pepper to taste

Thoroughly rinse the black-eyed peas. Place in a large pan with water to cover by at least 2 inches and soak overnight. (Quick-soak method: Bring peas to a boil, cover, and let stand for 1 hour.)

Drain soaking water from peas, and add the 2 quarts water. Add the onion, green pepper, celery, liquid smoke, and seitan. Season to taste. Bring to a boil, then reduce heat to medium-low and simmer, covered, for about 2 hours or until peas are tender enough to mash easily. Add water as needed while cooking. Serves 4.

El Pollo Loco Beans

Stuffed up? The hot peppers in this dish are a natural remedy. And if you suffer from arthritis, these peppers also provide relief for that by enhancing the blood flow throughout your body.

¼   cup corn oil
2   to 5 fresh serrano peppers, seeded and minced
2   teaspoons chili powder
1   small onion, diced
2   cups cooked pinto beans, or 24 ounces canned pintos, drained and rinsed
¾   cup water or vegetable stock
    Sea salt and pepper to taste

Heat oil in a large, nonreactive saucepan over medium heat and sauté the serrano chiles until tender. Add the remaining ingredients and stir to combine. Bring to a boil, reduce heat to low and simmer for 15 minutes. Serves 6.

Peppers such as jalapeños, habaneros, and serranos contain capsaicin, a colorless substance that gives the peppers their hotness. If you ever cook with such peppers, I believe a few words of caution are needed—and I speak from painful first-hand experience.

Early in my cooking career, I was told by the chef to clean, seed, and chop several pounds of jalapeño, scotch bonnet, and serrano peppers for a Southwestern-themed banquet at a large Boston restaurant. I was an arrogant and cocky thirty-something and wanted to impress the chef, so when he asked if I

knew how to prep and handle hot peppers, I answered, "Of course! Done it a thousand times."

On that particular day, I happened to have a whopper of a cold and my nose was running like a broken spigot. Nevertheless, we had only one hour to prepare for the banquet, so I just kept my head down, sniffling like crazy, and seeded and chopped away furiously—but without the protection of plastic gloves. After a while my runny nose got the better of me and I wiped it with my fingers. Within two minutes my nose was on fire, and, not knowing what was going on, I dashed to the men's room to check it out. Once I got there, despite the pain of my nose, I realized I also needed to avail myself of the facilities and proceeded to do so.

Well, to make a long story short, after a while the chef wondered where the heck I was and went looking for me. He found me in the men's room, my trousers around my ankles, dancing in circles in abject pain. Once he realized what had happened, his anger vanished and he roared with laughter. Not being a cruel man, though, he promptly summoned his sous chef to bring a cup of yogurt.

"Here, Mr. I-Know-Everything," the chef said as he handed me the yogurt. "Stick your . . . um, well . . . use this and the pain will go away, I promise. Trust me."

In desperation, I complied without hesitation and, sure enough, it worked. By that time, though, I had to endure the pain of humiliation, as the whole kitchen and wait staff had gathered to enjoy the spectacle.

The moral of this story: When working with hot peppers, always wear plastic gloves. And keep your fingers away from any and all sensitive body parts!

Mediterranean Garbanzo Beans

1 tablespoon extra virgin olive oil
4 green onions, chopped (white and green parts)
4 cloves garlic, minced
1 teaspoon crushed red pepper flakes
3 cups cooked garbanzo beans (or 2 cans, drained and rinsed)
1 10-ounce package frozen chopped spinach, defrosted and
    squeezed dry (or the equivalent of fresh spinach)
1 28-ounce can crushed tomatoes
1 cup diced fresh tomatoes (or 1 can diced tomatoes)
  Juice of one lemon
1 tablespoon capers
2 tablespoons chopped fresh oregano (or 1 teaspoon dried)
  Sea salt and black pepper to taste

In a skillet, heat the olive oil over medium heat and sauté the onions, garlic, and crushed red pepper flakes until the onions are tender. Add the garbanzos, spinach, and tomatoes.

Reduce heat to medium-low, cover the skillet, and simmer for 30 minutes, stirring occasionally. Add the lemon juice, capers, oregano, salt and pepper and serve. Serves 6.

Vegan Kidney Bean and Cashew Bonanza

2   tablespoons peanut or sunflower oil
3   ounces filberts, chopped
1/4 cup water
2   tablespoons chopped fresh tarragon
2   tablespoons chopped fresh basil
     Sea salt to taste
1   teaspoon curry powder
1   cup cooked brown rice
1   cup canned kidney beans, drained and rinsed
1/4 cup cashew pieces

Preheat oven to 375 degrees. Lightly grease a 9-by-13-inch baking dish with sunflower oil.

In the bowl of a food processor, combine the filberts, water, tarragon, basil, salt, and curry, and blend until a creamy sauce is achieved.

In a mixing bowl, combine the rice and beans. Add the filbert mixture and stir to blend. Pour the mixture into the prepared baking dish and bake for 15 minutes. Garnish with cashew pieces. Serves 4.

Basic Quinoa

The Quinoa Corporation notes that most varieties of quinoa (pronounced keen-wa) *have a naturally occurring bitter-tasting coating of saponin. This coating is usually removed prior to sale; however, there may be a small amount of bitter residue or powder left on the grain, which can be removed simply by rinsing before cooking.*

1 cup quinoa
2 cups water
1 pinch sea salt

Rinse the quinoa several times and drain well. Place the two cups of water and salt in a 1-quart saucepan and bring it to a boil. Stirring, add the quinoa, reduce the heat to medium, cover and simmer for at about 15 minutes, or until all the liquid is absorbed. Garnish at will. If you have any leftovers, store them covered in the refrigerator for up to 5 days. Makes 3 cups.

Quinoa Pilaf

6	cups cooked quinoa
1/2	cup diced carrot
1/2	cup sliced green onion
1/4	cup diced celery
1/4	cup diced green bell pepper
1/4	cup diced red bell pepper
1/4	cup butter or olive oil
2	cloves garlic, chopped
1	cup sliced almonds
1/4	teaspoon oregano
	Sea salt and pepper to taste

Toast the almonds, dry, in a heavy skillet over medium-high heat, just until lightly golden brown. (This takes only a short time—if you can smell 'em, they're done!) Set aside.

In a skillet over medium heat, heat the oil and sauté vegetables until onions are translucent (veggies should still be crisp). Stir in the oregano. Add the sautéed vegetables to the cooked quinoa, mixing well. Add salt and pepper to taste. Add almonds and toss to mix. Garnish with fresh oregano leaves. Serves 6–8.

Adapted from a recipe from Quinoa Corporation,
Ancient Harvest, Gardena, California.

Pressure-Cooked Brown Rice

    2   cups long- or medium-grain brown rice
2$\frac{1}{2}$ cups water
  $\frac{1}{4}$ teaspoon sea salt

Thoroughly rinse the rice, drain, and place it and the water and salt in a pressure cooker. Cover securely according to directions and bring the pressure up to high. Reduce heat according to directions and cook for 45–60 minutes.

PRESSURE-COOKER NOVICES: Be sure the pressure is high enough to create a gentle hissing throughout the cooking process. Serves 4.

Basic Brown Rice Pilaf

*Around our home, this is the most common vegetarian
"comfort" meal. The marvelous dish is quite simple, full of
nutrients—and it's colon-cleansing, to boot, full of both
soluble and insoluble fiber. Besides rice, it can be prepared
with millet, quinoa, barley, or any of your favorite grains.*

3	tablespoons extra virgin olive oil
1	medium onion, chopped
1	clove garlic, minced
1/4	cup cashew pieces, toasted
2	carrots, finely diced
1	red bell pepper, finely diced
1	cup julienned fresh shiitake mushrooms
4	cups cooked brown rice
1	cup cooked legumes of your choice
2	eggs, lightly beaten, or 1/2 cup liquid egg substitute
	Sea salt and cracked fresh pepper to taste
	Chopped parsley

Heat the oil in a large skillet over medium heat. Stir in the onion,
garlic, cashews, carrots, pepper, and shiitakes. Sauté, stirring
frequently, until the veggies begin to soften and the onions are just
beginning to brown. Remove all these goodies to a bowl and set aside
(but keep it warm).

You want to keep the flavors, so don't wipe out that pan! Place the
pan back on medium heat and pour in the eggs or egg substitute.
Cook, stirring constantly until the eggs are lightly scrambled.

Add the veggie mixture to the eggs and add the brown rice. Gently
mix together. Serve garnished with parsley, and, if you like, with a
dash of low-sodium soy sauce (or Bragg Liquid Aminos) for a little
added flavor. Serves 4.

American Fried Rice

This is an alternative to the greasy restaurant versions.
Next time you eat in an Asian restaurant, remember that
generally speaking, fried rice was created to get rid of
kitchen leftover bits of meat and veggies.

2   cups cooked brown rice
2   eggs or ½ cup liquid egg substitute
2   tablespoons peanut oil
1   cup diced tempeh or meat substitute
½   cup thinly sliced celery
1   cup diced onion
1   teaspoon minced garlic
2   tablespoons chopped red pepper
½   cup frozen peas, thawed
4   tablespoons dry-roasted peanuts
3   tablespoons soy sauce
2   drops liquid smoke
    Vegetable stock
    Sea salt to taste
    Chopped green onion, parsley, and cilantro

Spritz a sauté pan with a bit of vegetable cooking spray, and over medium heat scramble the eggs or egg substitute. Set aside.

In another sauté pan, heat the peanut oil over medium-high heat. Add the rice and brown it slowly, shaking the skillet back and forth and stirring to keep the rice moving around. Reduce the heat to medium and add the tempeh or meat substitute, celery, onion, garlic, red pepper, and peanuts. Sauté for 1 minute then add the soy sauce, liquid smoke, and scrambled egg. Continue stirring to keep things mixed up so it all gets hot.

If the dish seems a little dry, add a little stock to moisten it as you desire and cook, stirring, for 3 more minutes. Add the peas and adjust spices. Garnish with the chopped green onion, parsley, and cilantro. Serves 4.

Spicy Mexican Rice

A fast, simple and satisfying dish kids will love. In fact, why not let the kids help out, for a great bonding experience?

³/₄	cups water
¹/₂	cup instant brown rice
	Sea salt and black pepper to taste
2	teaspoons ground cumin
¹/₄	teaspoon cinnamon
¹/₄	teaspoon (scant) cayenne
1	tablespoon chili powder
1	poblano or green bell pepper, diced
1	medium onion, diced
2	teaspoons peanut oil
¹/₃	cup hulled green pumpkin seeds
2	tablespoons minced cilantro

In a medium saucepan, bring water to a boil and add the rice. Cover the pan, reduce the heat to low, and simmer for 10 minutes or until liquid is absorbed. Add the salt and pepper, cumin, cinnamon, cayenne, and chili powder. Set aside.

In a large skillet, heat the oil over medium heat and add the pumpkin seeds. Toast them for about 3 minutes, stirring frequently. Transfer seeds to a paper towel to drain the oil.

Fluff the rice with a fork and stir in pumpkin seeds and cilantro. Serves 2–4.

Gingered Barley

  1   cup pearled barley, rinsed and drained
  3   tablespoons extra virgin olive oil, divided use
 ½   teaspoon salt
  1   teaspoon fennel powder
 ½   teaspoon anise
 ⅛   teaspoon ground cloves
 ¼   cup raisins
      Peel of 1 orange (orange part only!), julienned
2¼   cups water
  2   tablespoons minced fresh ginger
  2   cups grated butternut squash
  2   stalks celery, chopped
  3   tablespoons toasted sesame seeds

Place the barley in a large saucepan and drizzle with 1½ tablespoons of the olive oil. Add the salt, fennel, anise, cloves, orange peel, and raisins. Add the water and stir. Bring to a boil, then lower the heat to medium-low, cover the pot, and simmer slowly for 45 minutes or until the water has been absorbed. Remove the orange peel.

In a large skillet, over medium fire, heat the remaining oil. Add the garlic, ginger, squash, celery, and onions and stir just to combine. Cover the skillet and let the veggies steam slightly, just until tender. Stir frequently.

Fold the vegetable mixture into the cooked barley, and adjust the seasonings to taste. Garnish with the toasted sesame seeds. Serves 6.

Asian "Beef" Noodle Salad

4 ounces whole-wheat noodles
2 teaspoons toasted sesame seed oil
8 ounces "fake" beef (vegetarian meat substitute), cut into
      strips
1 cup snow peas
½ cup julienne-cut carrots
½ cup low-sodium teriyaki sauce
2 tablespoons lime juice
2 teaspoons chili garlic sauce
1 tablespoon fresh minced ginger
6 cups torn spinach, lightly packed
¼ cup chopped fresh cilantro

Cook noodles per instructions; drain and keep warm.

Heat the sesame oil in a sauté pan over high heat, then add the meat substitute, peas, and carrots. Stir-fry until the veggies just begin to soften.

Add all remaining ingredients except spinach and cilantro. Continue stir-frying until thoroughly heated. Add the noodles; toss well. Place the spinach in a large bowl and top with the stir-fry. Garnish with cilantro. Serves 6.

Singapore Noodles

This is one of my wife's favorite Asian dishes.

    2   tablespoons rice wine vinegar
    2   teaspoons minced ginger
  $1/2$ teaspoon toasted sesame seed oil
    1   pound tempeh, finely diced
  $1/2$ cup vegetable stock
    2   tablespoons water
  $1/2$ teaspoon sweetener
    1   teaspoon each sea salt and black pepper
  $3^1/2$ tablespoons vegetable oil
$1^1/2$ tablespoons curry powder
  $3^1/2$ cups thinly sliced leeks
$1^1/2$ tablespoons minced ginger
    3   cups bean sprouts
    4   ounces thin Chinese noodles, cooked according to package
        directions and drained

Combine the rice wine vinegar, 2 teaspoons ginger, and sesame seed oil. Add the tempeh and marinade for several hours.

Combine the vegetable stock, water, sweetener, salt, and pepper. Mix well and set aside.

Heat 2 tablespoons of the vegetable oil in a skillet over medium-high heat. Add the tempeh and stir-fry until golden brown.

Remove the tempeh and wipe the pan with a clean paper towel. Add the remaining vegetable oil and the curry powder to the pan and stir-fry until fragrant. Add the leeks and $1^1/2$ tablespoons ginger and stir-fry for about 1–2 minutes, or until the leeks are somewhat tender. Add the bean sprouts and cook for about another 30 seconds. Add the tempeh, noodles, and vegetable stock mixture. Gently toss until noodles have absorbed the sauce and are tender. Serves 6.

Note: Because of their high fat and calorie content, I don't recommend using ramen noodles in this recipe.

Shiitake Noodles

2	tablespoons low-sodium soy sauce
1	tablespoon honey
2	tablespoons toasted sesame oil
1	tablespoon peanut oil
1	tablespoons minced garlic
1	tablespoon minced fresh ginger
4	green onions, chopped
1	teaspoon crushed red pepper flakes
1	pound fresh shiitake mushrooms, cleaned and slivered
1/2	pound fresh snow peas
1	bunch cilantro, chopped
1	pound Asian noodles (Eden Brand Organic Brown Rice or Buckwheat preferred), cooked according to package directions
	Toasted peanut or cashew pieces

Blend the soy, honey, and sesame oil in a small mixing bowl.

In a wok or large skillet, heat the peanut oil over medium-high heat and sauté the garlic, ginger, green onions, and crushed red pepper flakes over medium high heat. Cook just until the garlic begins to brown (don't let the garlic burn!), stirring constantly.

Add the shiitakes and snow peas and stir-fry for another 2 minutes. Don't walk away from the stove—stay put!

Add the noodles and stir until the mixture is warm. Add the cilantro and soy-honey sauce, and lightly toss to blend. Serve topped with toasted peanuts or cashews if you wish. Serves 4.

Yakisoba

1 package Chinese noodles
1 teaspoon toasted sesame oil
4 ounces meat substitute
1 tablespoon minced garlic
Pinch of crushed red pepper flakes (optional)
1 tablespoon minced ginger
2 cups thinly sliced cabbage or shredded slaw mix
1 cup finely diced vegetables
1 medium onion, thinly sliced
3 tablespoons Worcestershire sauce
2 tablespoons soy sauce
2 tablespoons chopped cilantro
1 green onion, chopped
Pickled ginger

Cook the noodles according to package directions. Drain and set aside.

In a skillet, heat the sesame oil over medium heat. Add the meat substitute, garlic, crushed red pepper flakes, and ginger. Stir and simmer until the garlic begins to turn golden; add the cabbage, diced vegetables, and sliced onions. Increase heat to medium-high and stir-fry until cabbage wilts and onions are soft. Don't walk away for even a moment—this all happens rather quickly and it would be easy to burn the dish.

Reduce heat to medium-low and add the drained noodles, Worcestershire, soy sauce, cilantro, and green onions, and toss gently. Garnish with a little pile of pickled ginger. Serve hot. Serves 2.

Casseroles and Entrees

The thought manifests as the word,
The word manifests as the deed,
The deed develops into habit,
The habit hardens into character.
So watch the thought and its ways with care,
And let it spring from love
Born of our concern for all beings.

—Buddha

Shepherd's Pie

Grab a glass of your favorite hearty dry red wine to compliment this tasty version of the traditional hamburger-based classic

3	tablespoons Smart Balance Buttery Spread
1	medium onion, diced
1	stalk celery, diced
1	carrot, diced
2	portabella mushrooms, diced
3	cloves garlic, finely minced
1½	cups dry red wine
1½	cups vegetable stock
¼	cup tomato paste
	Sea salt and freshly cracked black pepper to taste
2	tablespoons minced fresh oregano, or 1 teaspoon dried
1	cup frozen peas
1	tablespoon balsamic vinegar
3	cups of your favorite garlic mashed potato recipe
1	cup cooked brown rice

Preheat oven to 425 degrees. Spritz a casserole dish with cooking spray.

Heat 2 tablespoons of the Smart Balance Buttery Spread in a large skillet over medium-high heat. Sauté the onion, celery, and carrots until onions are translucent. Lower the heat to medium-low and add the garlic. Cook for about another minute—don't burn that garlic! Add the remaining Smart Balance Buttery Spread and the mushrooms and cook 3–4 minutes. Add the wine and vegetable stock. Stir in the tomato paste and salt and pepper and simmer gently for 15 minutes, stirring frequently. Add the basil, peas, and balsamic vinegar.

Pour the mixture into the prepared casserole dish. Carefully cover the entire top with the mashed potatoes and bake for 20 minutes or until the top begins to brown. Serves 6.

New Old-Fashioned Goulash Casserole

The woodsy, meaty shiitake mushrooms in this classic dish not only taste fantastic, but will also spur your immune system! Nothing spells lovin' like somethin' from your oven!

4   cups whole-wheat elbow macaroni
1   pound soy ground meat substitute
8   ounces shiitake mushrooms, stemmed and thinly sliced
2   tablespoons finely minced garlic
2   medium onions, chopped
1   10-ounce can crushed tomatoes
2   14-ounce cans diced tomatoes, undrained (or chop up 3 or 4
        fresh tomatoes from the garden! For added juiciness,
        peel one tomato and puree it in the food processor or
        blender then add it to the diced tomatoes. Great flavor!)
1   tablespoon sweet Hungarian paprika
    Sea salt and cracked black pepper to taste

Preheat oven to 350 degrees. Cook macaroni just until al dente, drain, and set aside. Meanwhile, cook meat substitute according to package directions. Add shiitakes, garlic, and onion and cook until onions are translucent. Add crushed tomatoes and diced tomatoes, paprika, and salt and pepper, and cook for another 3–5 minutes, stirring frequently. Add pasta and pour into 3-quart glass casserole. Bake for 40–50 minutes until bubbly. Serves 6.

Savory Sauerkraut and Barley Casserole

*Make this hearty and warming dish in advance and freeze
what's left for a rainy-day supper, when you'd rather be
reading a good book than stand in the kitchen.*

3   pounds seitan (or other wheat meat substitute)
1/2   cup water
3   cups dry red wine
1/2   cup mushroom soy sauce
2   quarts sauerkraut, drained
1   large white or yellow onion, thinly sliced
1   cup pearled barley, rinsed and drained
2   bay leaves
1   teaspoon freshly cracked black pepper
4   drops liquid smoke
4   cups water

Preheat oven to 350 degrees.

In a large pot, combine the 1/2 cup water, red wine, and mushroom soy sauce. Add the seitan, cover, and simmer for 5 minutes. Let cool, then cut the seitan into bite-size pieces. Reserve the cooking liquid.

Place seitan in a dutch oven or large casserole. Layer the sauerkraut and onion over the seitan, and sprinkle the barley over the kraut. Tuck in the bay leaves and sprinkle on the pepper. Mix the liquid smoke with the quart of water, then pour over the seitan and kraut mixture. Cover and bake for 3 hours—if you can stand to wait that long. The aroma will drive you mad! If the casserole gets too dry, add the reserved cooking liquid from the seitan as needed. Serves 8–10.

Vegetarian Swiss Steak

This dish's flavor and aroma transports me back to the wonderful days of my youth and Mom's Sunday-dinner Swiss steak. Seitan is a high-gluten meat substitute made from wheat; its taste and texture are hearty enough to satisfy any carnivore. Serve this crowd-pleaser over whole wheat pasta or brown rice, accompanied by a fresh green salad.

¹/₂	cup white wine or water
1	large onion, halved and thinly sliced
3	cups sliced mushrooms
2	stalks celery, chopped
1	large green bell pepper, diced
1	red bell pepper, diced (optional)
2	tablespoons minced garlic (about 6–8 large cloves)
2	tablespoons chopped fresh basil, or 2 teaspoons dried
¹/₄	cup light miso dissolved in ¹/₂ cup water
1	28-ounce can diced tomatoes
1	tablespoon tomato concentrate
	Sea salt and black pepper to taste
16	ounces seitan (wheat meat), cut into thick slices

Preheat oven to 350 degrees.

Heat the wine or water in a large skillet or pot, add the onion and braise until it is soft, about 5 minutes. Add the mushrooms, peppers, garlic, and basil. Continue cooking over medium heat for 8 to 10 minutes, then stir in the dissolved miso, tomatoes, and pepper. Simmer 5 minutes.

Spread ¹/₂ cup of the sauce evenly in the bottom of a large casserole dish. Arrange the seitan slices in the dish, and then cover with the rest of the sauce. Cover the dish and bake 20–25 minutes. Serves 8.

"Meaty" Veggie Pot Roast

After more than a decade of vegetarianism, I still occasionally crave some of the comfort foods of my boyhood and the texture of meat, so I came up with this Sunday after-church classic.

2   teaspoons extra virgin olive oil
1   large onion, coarsely chopped
2   pounds seitan ("wheat meat") or veggie burgers
4   carrots, thinly sliced
4   small Yukon Gold potatoes, quartered (don't peel 'em!)
2   stalks celery, diced
1   cup Mushroom Gravy (recipe follows)
1   bay leaf
$^1/_2$ cup dry red wine
2   tablespoons tomato paste

Preheat oven to 350 degrees.

Heat the olive oil in a large skillet over medium heat, add onion, and sauté until translucent. Add the seitan or veggie burgers and cook just until heated through.

Place the meat substitute and onion mixture in a baking dish along with the carrots, potatoes, and celery. Prepare the Mushroom Gravy and add the wine, tomato paste, and bay leaf. Pour the mixture over the meat substitute and vegetables and bake 30–45 minutes. Serves 4.

Mushroom Gravy

4   tablespoons extra virgin olive oil
1   medium onion, finely chopped
1   medium carrot, unpeeled, grated

1	celery stalk, finely diced
1	bay leaf
2	cups thinly sliced mushrooms (stems, too)
6	cups vegetable stock
1	can tomato paste
1/4	cup mushroom soy sauce
1	cup dry red wine
3	tablespoons cornstarch
3	tablespoons water

In a large pot, heat the olive oil over medium-high heat. Add the onion, carrot, celery, bay leaf, and mushrooms, and sauté for about 3 minutes. Add the vegetable stock, tomato paste, soy sauce, and wine. Bring just to a boil, then reduce heat and simmer for 4 minutes.

Whisk the cornstarch into the water and add to the simmering sauce a bit at a time, stirring constantly and taking care not to over-thicken. Makes about 6 cups.

Vegetarian Stroganoff

*There are wonderful reduced-fat and nonfat sour creams
out there nowadays—be adventurous and give one a try.
Life is too short to live without sour cream, as long as
we practice moderation.*

  1 tablespoon vegetable oil
  1 tablespoon olive oil
  1 package meat substitute, cut into strips
1½ pounds mushrooms (stems included), cleaned and sliced
  1 bay leaf
  1 tablespoon thyme
  1 teaspoon minced garlic
  1 medium onion, diced
  2 cans water chestnuts, cut into quarters
  1 medium sweet potato, scrubbed and cut into ½-inch cubes
  1 teaspoon sea salt
  1 stalk celery, diced
  2 cups frozen peas
  2 cups bite-size cauliflower florets
  1 tablespoon cornstarch
 ½ cup dry sherry or Marsala wine
  2 tablespoons mushroom soy sauce
  1 cup reduced-fat or nonfat sour cream
     Chopped parsley

Heat the vegetable and olive oils in a sauté pan over medium heat.
Add the meat substitute, mushrooms, bay leaf, thyme, celery,
cauliflower, garlic, onion, water chestnuts, and sweet potato. Cook,
covered, for about 5 minutes, stirring every now and then. Cook over
medium for about 5 minutes, or until the sweet potato and
cauliflower are tender.

Dissolve the cornstarch in the sherry or Marsala wine. Add to the meat mixture and cook, stirring, for 1 minute or until sauce slightly thickens.

Mix in the sour cream, and serve over a bed of grains or whole grain pasta. Garnish with chopped parsley. Serves 4.

Cheese and Green Chile Enchiladas

  1 package extra-firm tofu, drained, press-dried, and cut into small pieces
  1 cup fresh or frozen (thawed) corn kernels
  2 cups salsa, use divided
1¼ cup low-fat grated jack or mozzarella cheese, use divided
  1 4-ounce can diced green chiles
  ¾ cup chopped Spanish or black olives, use divided
  1 cup chopped cilantro, use divided
  8 soft flour tortillas (8-inch size)
  1 10-ounce can or jar enchilada sauce

Preheat oven to 450 degrees. Lightly coat a 13-by-9-inch baking dish with vegetable cooking spray.

In a large bowl, combine the tofu, corn, 1 cup of salsa, ¾ cup of the cheese, the chiles, ½ cup olives, and 4 tablespoons of the cilantro. Mix, taking care to not break up the tofu.

Spoon a portion of the mixture onto the lower third of a tortilla. Roll the tortilla fairly tightly and place seam-side-down into the prepared baking dish. Repeat with the remaining tortillas and mixture. Pour the enchilada sauce over the enchiladas and sprinkle with the remaining cheese and olives. Bake 20–30 minutes or until bubbly and the cheese is golden. Remove from oven and let sit for about 5 minutes. Serve topped with the remaining salsa and cilantro. Serves 8.

Broccoli Casserole, New Millennium Style

Lucky for us, my gentle, soft-spoken Aunt Bernie shared this recipe with her close friends and family. Since we're aware now that "plastic" cheeses such as Velveeta are hazardous to our cardiovascular systems, I've made a minor change or two, subtly converting this classic dish into a heart-healthy casserole: Low cholesterol, low fat, high fiber, and chock full of protective phytonutrients.

6	butter or Smart Balance Buttery Spread, divided use
1/4	cup chopped onion
2	tablespoons organic unbleached all-purpose flour
1/2	cup water
8	ounces shredded cheddar (or soy cheddar cheese)
10	ounces fresh broccoli florets, blanched (frozen is fine, but drain it well)
3	eggs or 3/4 cup liquid egg substitute
1/2	cup whole grain bread crumbs

Preheat over to 325 degrees. Spritz a 1½-quart casserole with vegetable cooking spray.

Melt 4 tablespoons of the butter in a sauté pan over medium heat and cook onions until translucent. Stir in flour and cook, stirring, for about 2 minutes. Add water and continue cooking, stirring, until the mixture thickens and just comes to a boil. Add the cheese and broccoli and continue cooking until cheese melts. Add egg substitute and gently incorporate.

Pour this nourishing glop into the prepared dish. Top with breadcrumbs and dot with the remaining Smart Balance Buttery Spread. Bake for 30 minutes. Serves 8.

Spaghetti Florentine Casserole

2   eggs or ½ cup liquid egg substitute
2   tablespoons chopped onion
1   cup nonfat sour cream
1   cup plain soymilk (or low-fat milk)
1   teaspoon sea salt
    Pinch of nutmeg
    Fresh cracked pepper to taste
¼   cup grated Parmesan cheese or soy Parmesan, divided use
2   cups shredded Monterey jack cheese
2   10-ounce packages frozen chopped spinach, thawed and
        squeezed dry
4   tablespoons wheat germ
8   ounces whole wheat spaghetti, cooked al dente

Preheat oven to 350 degrees and spritz your favorite 2-quart casserole dish with vegetable cooking spray.

In a large bowl, combine eggs or egg substitute, onion, sour cream, soymilk or milk, salt, nutmeg, pepper, two tablespoons of the Parmesan, the jack cheese, and wheat germ. Mix well.

Fold in the spinach and cooked pasta. Pour the mixture in the prepared baking dish and sprinkle with remaining Parmesan. Bake covered for 15 minutes; remove cover and bake for another 15 minutes until lightly browned. Serves 4.

Spinach-Rice Casserole with Veggies

4 cups cooked brown rice

1 tablespoon extra virgin olive oil

1 tablespoon Dijon mustard

1 cup chopped spinach, cooked (or frozen, thawed), well drained

1 medium onion, diced

1¹/₃ cup water chestnuts

¹/₂ cup diced red pepper

¹/₂ cup chopped celery

¹/₃ cup low-sodium soy sauce

Cracked black pepper to taste

²/₃ cup crushed reduced-fat potato chips or whole wheat breadcrumbs

Preheat oven to 350 degrees. Spray a casserole dish with vegetable spray.

Combine all ingredients except potato chips or breadcrumbs and pour into prepared dish. Top with the chips or breadcrumbs. Bake uncovered for 30 minutes. Serves 4.

Jerked Tempeh

1   cup apple juice
3   tablespoon grated onion
3   cloves garlic, minced
2   tablespoons soy sauce
    As much habañero pepper or your favorite fresh, hot pepper as
      you can handle, minced
2   tablespoons red wine vinegar
1   tablespoon grated ginger
1   teaspoon allspice
$^{1}/_{2}$ teaspooon cinnamon
4   drops liquid smoke
    Freshly ground black pepper to taste
1   teaspoon dry thyme
1   teaspoon freshly grated nutmeg
1   pound tempeh (steam with your veggie steamer for 10
      minutes)
1   cup chopped green onions

Combine the apple juice, onion, garlic, soy sauce, hot peppers, vinegar, ginger, allspice, cinnamon, liquid smoke, black pepper, thyme, and nutmeg in a blender or food processor, and process just until blended.

Meanwhile, steam the tempeh for 10 minutes (use your veggie steamer). Cut the tempeh into 1-inch cubes and arrange in a layer in a baking dish. Pour the blended mix over the tempeh and work it in with your hands. Let marinate at least 2 hours or overnight.

Preheat your grill, oven broiler, or even a countertop grill, if you have one. Broil the tempeh nuggets for 5 minutes, turn, and continue broiling for another 5 minutes. Serve hot with some whole grains and garnish with the chopped green onions. The tempeh makes great leftovers as super sandwich fillings. Serves 4.

Whole Wheat Pizza Dough

Haul out the pizza stone—it's time to make pizza!

1½ cups warm water (about 110 degrees)
1 teaspoon honey
1 package active dry yeast
2 tablespoons extra virgin olive oil
2 cups unbleached white flour
1 tablespoon wheat germ
1 teaspoon sea salt
1½ cups whole wheat flour

Combine the water and honey and add the yeast, stirring gently just until the yeast is dissolved. Stir in the olive oil and set aside.

Combine the white flour, wheat germ, and salt in a large mixing bowl, making a well in the center. Add the yeast mixture and stir with a wooden spoon just until blended. Gradually stir in the whole wheat flour, adding only enough to make a soft, workable dough.

Turn the dough out onto a lightly floured surface and knead until smooth and elastic, about 5 minutes. The dough should be slightly tacky but not sticky. Place the dough in an olive oil-coated bowl, cover with a damp towel, and let rise in a warm place until it has doubled in bulk, about 60 minutes. Punch down and shape. Top with your choice of toppings and bake in a preheated oven at 400 degrees about 15 minutes, or until dough is crispy. Makes one 16-inch pizza or 6 small pizza pockets.

Side Dishes

Send Thy peace O Lord, which is perfect and everlasting,
that our souls may radiate peace.
Send Thy peace O Lord, that we may think, act and speak
harmoniously.
Send Thy peace O Lord, that we may be contented and
thankful for Thy bountiful gifts.
Send Thy peace O Lord, that amidst our worldly strife, we
may enjoy Thy bliss.
Send Thy peace O Lord, that we may endure all, tolerate
all, in the thought of Thy grace and mercy.
Send Thy peace O Lord, that our lives may become a Divine
vision and in Thy light, all darkness may vanish.
Send Thy peace O Lord, our Father and Mother, that we Thy
children on Earth may all unite in one family.

— "Prayer for Peace," Pir-o-Murshid Inayat Khan, 1921

Eureka Gold Potatoes

Often, the best dishes come around by mistake. This dish is one of those. One day I happened to mix up some smashed potatoes and cooked millet. It tasted pretty good, but it was missing something, so I added some blanched cauliflower to ramp up the flavor. My kitchen staff thought I was crazy, but after one taste, they were hooked.

The addition of millet to smashed potatoes shoots the nutritional value right up the charts. Loaded with protein, folate, and B vitamins, millet is considered by some heath professionals to be the most nutritious cereal grain in the world. And to think, for all we knew, it was just for the birds!

¼	cup extra virgin olive oil or Smart Balance Buttery Spread
3	cloves garlic, minced
¼	cup minced onion
½	head cauliflower, very finely chopped
2	cups warm smashed potatoes
2	cups cooked millet
½	cup vegetable stock
3	tablespoons low-fat milk or plain soymilk (optional)
½	cup chopped fresh parsley
	Sea salt and pepper to taste

In a large saucepan, heat the oil or Smart Balance over medium heat. Add the garlic, onion, and cauliflower and sauté for 3–5 minutes, or until the onion is translucent and the cauliflower is tender. Stir in the millet and remove from heat, but keep it warm.

In a small saucepan, combine the milk and vegetable stock. Heat over medium heat; do not boil.

In a large bowl, combine the smashed potatoes and millet mixture,

stirring gently until well-blended. Add the milk and vegetable stock a bit at a time until the mixture is the desired consistency. (Don't overmix or you'll end up with something like gummy wallpaper paste!) Add salt and pepper as desired and serve with pride. Serves 4.

Mashed Potatoes and Cabbage

1   pound new red potatoes, scrubbed (leave 'em in their jackets, Jack!)
$3/4$ pound white or savoy cabbage, shredded
1   bunch fresh chives, chopped
$3/4$ cup nonfat buttermilk or plain kefir
2   teaspoons Dijon mustard
     Sea salt and pepper to taste

Place the potatoes in a large pot with just enough water to cover. Bring to a boil and cook for 15 minutes or until tender. Drain and smash with a potato masher. (Don't over-mash—a few lumps are good!)

Meanwhile, in another pot, steam the cabbage for about 5 minutes, until it wilts. Drain and add to the smashed potatoes. Add the buttermilk or kefir, mustard, and salt and pepper. Combine thoroughly and serve. Serves 2.

Give Peas a Chance!

Au Gratin Potatoes

   1   tablespoon olive oil or Smart Balance Buttery Spread
1½   pounds new red potatoes, scrubbed and thinly sliced
   3   cloves garlic, minced
¼   cup wheat germ
½   cup low-fat grated sharp cheddar cheese
1½   cup reconstituted nonfat dry milk (add more of the dry milk
       to taste to make it extra-strong)
     Sea salt and black pepper to taste

Preheat oven to 350 degrees. Grease a shallow ovenproof baking dish with the olive oil or Smart Balance. In a large bowl, combine the remaining ingredients. Pour into the prepared baking dish and bake, uncovered, for 35–40 minutes, or until golden brown. Serves 4.

Hungarian Cabbage and Potatoes

2 tablespoons vegetable oil
1 large onion, diced
3 garlic cloves, minced
1 medium head of cabbage, shredded
4 cups vegetable stock
3 large russet potatoes, unpeeled and diced
1 teaspoon paprika
1/4 teaspoon ground cumin
   Sea salt and black pepper to taste
2 tablespoons cornstarch
1/2 cup chopped fresh parsley

In a large pan, heat 1 tablespoon of oil and sauté the onion and garlic until tender. Add the shredded cabbage and sauté until the cabbage begins to soften. Add the vegetable stock, potatoes, paprika, cumin, and salt and pepper and bring to a boil. Reduce the heat to medium-low, cover, and simmer for 30 minutes.

Combine the remaining 1 tablespoon of oil and the cornstarch. Blend it into the cabbage and potato mixture. Cook, stirring, about 5 minutes or until slightly thickened. Garnish with parsley. Serves 6–8.

Creole Cabbage

*This is great served over whole grains accompanied
by a dark green leafy salad.*

1	tablespoon olive oil
1/2	cup diced celery
2	cups shredded cabbage
1/4	cup chopped onions
1/2	cup diced red pepper
1/2	cup diced green bell pepper
1	cup diced tomatoes
2	sprigs of fresh thyme
1/8	teaspoon cayenne pepper
1	tablespoon Dijon mustard
1	tablespoon sour mash whiskey
3/4	teaspoon sea salt
1/2	teaspoon Sucanat

In a large, heavy skillet, heat the olive oil over medium-low heat. Add the remaining ingredients and stir well. Cover and cook 10–12 minutes, stirring occasionally. Be careful not to overcook. Remove the thyme sprigs and serve. Serves 4.

Sweet and Sour Red Cabbage

*The cooking method used here is called braising,
which is an old-fashioned way of slow cooking with
liquid. The combination of spices and apples will
make your house smell terrific!*

2	tablespoons butter or Smart Balance Buttery Spread
2	tablespoons olive oil
2	medium onions, diced
4	Granny Smith apples, unpeeled, chopped
4	tablespoon raisins
4	tablespoon Sucanat
$1/2$	teaspoon ground cloves
1	teaspoon cinnamon
3	tablespoons lemon juice
1	medium head red cabbage, shredded
1	cup dry white wine
2	cups apple juice or cider
2	bay leaves

In a large pan, heat the butter and oil over medium heat. Add the onions and sauté until soft and translucent. Add the apples, raisins, Sucanat, cloves, cinnamon, and lemon juice. Cook for about 10 minutes, until the apples are tender.

Add the shredded cabbage and wine and sauté for about another 5 minutes. Add the apple juice and bay leaves, cover, and cook over low heat for 30 minutes. Serves 8–10.

Broiled Cauliflower and Broccoli

¹/₂   pound broccoli florets (fresh or frozen)
¹/₂   pound cauliflower florets (fresh or frozen)
 2   tablespoons olive oil
 4   tablespoons Smart Balance Buttery Spread
 2   teaspoons grated ginger
 2   tablespoons wheat germ
      Juice and zest (yellow part only, grated) of ¹/₂ lemon
 4   tablespoons chopped fresh cilantro
 2   green onions, chopped
      Sea salt and pepper to taste
¹/₄   cup grated sharp cheddar cheese

Preheat the broiler.

Cook the broccoli and cauliflower in the microwave with just a little waster, covered with a damp towel (or cook on the stovetop in a small amount of water) for 5–8 minutes, or just until tender. Drain well and transfer to a shallow ovenproof baking dish. Set aside, keeping it warm.

In a saucepan, heat the olive oil and Smart Balance Buttery Spread over medium heat until the Smart Balance Buttery Spread melts. Add the grated ginger, wheat germ, and lemon juice and zest, and simmer gently for 2–3 minutes, stirring frequently. Add the cilantro, green onion, and salt and pepper. Pour the mixture over the broccoli and cauliflower and sprinkle the cheese evenly over the top. Broil 8–10 inches from the broiler element, to avoid burning, just until the mixture begins to bubble and become golden. Serves 4.

Greek Green Beans

1   tablespoon olive oil
3   cloves garlic, crushed
1   pound green beans, blanched
2   cups vegetable stock
1   bay leaf
2   sprigs fresh oregano
1   tablespoon tomato paste
    Juice of one lemon
1   small red onion, chopped
1   ounce pitted Greek olives
$1/2$ cup chopped fresh parsley
    Sea salt and pepper to taste

In a saucepan, heat the olive oil over medium heat. Add the crushed garlic and sauté 4–5 minutes, or until the garlic just begins to brown. Add the beans, stock, bay leaf, oregano, tomato paste, lemon juice, and red onion; cover, and simmer for 1 hour, or until sauce is thickened. Stir in the olives and parsley, season with salt and pepper, and serve. Serves 4.

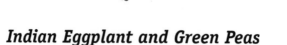

Indian Eggplant and Green Peas

1	tablespoon olive oil
2	teaspoons whole cumin seeds
1	medium onion, cut in half and thinly sliced
1	teaspoon sea salt, divided use
4	cloves garlic, minced
3	Japanese eggplants, cut into bite-size cubes
½	teaspoon cayenne pepper
½	mango, pureed
½	cup fresh or thawed frozen peas
¼	cup chopped cilantro

Heat oil in a heavy pan over medium high. Add the cumin seeds and sauté just until the seeds start to darken and become fragrant. Add the onion and ½ teaspoon salt and sauté until the onion starts to brown. Add the garlic and sauté 1 minute, then add the eggplant.

When the eggplant starts to soften (it won't take very long), add just enough water to prevent sticking. Add the remaining salt and cayenne. Reduce heat to low, cover the pan, and cook for 5 minutes, or until eggplant is done. Add the mango puree and peas and stir to combine. Garnish with the cilantro and serve over your grain of choice: brown rice, barley, quinoa, or millet. Serves 2.

Curried Spinach

If you're in a hurry for curry . . .

1½   pounds fresh spinach or chard
  1   tablespoon olive oil
  ¼   teaspoon Madras curry powder
  1   teaspoon mustard seed
  1   tablespoon tomato paste
  2   green onions, sliced

Remove the stems from the spinach or chard; wash thoroughly and drain.

Heat the oil in a large skillet over medium-high heat. Toss in the curry and mustard seeds and cover the pan quickly because those mustard seeds will pop.

Once the mustard seeds stop popping, add the onions, spinach or chard, and tomato paste. Stir the greens nonstop until they're wilted. Reduce the heat to medium-low, cover the skillet again, and continue cooking the greens for about 10 minutes or until most of the juices have evaporated. (You can use frozen spinach if you wish. It will not take as long to cook.)

Transfer to a warm dish and serve while hot. Serves 4.

Spinach Bake Casserole

*Popeye would like you to bake this traditional dish earlier
in the day and gently warm it for supper.*

1	10-ounce package frozen spinach, thawed and squeezed fairly dry
1/2	teaspoon sea salt
1/3	cup nonfat milk or plain soymilk
1	cup cooked brown rice
3	tablespoons chopped onion
2	tablespoons Smart Balance Buttery Spread or olive oil
2	eggs, lightly beaten, or 1/2 cup liquid egg substitute
1/2	teaspoon Worcestershire or Bragg Liquid Aminos
1	cup low-fat shredded cheddar or soy cheese
1	tablespoon fresh rosemary, minced
1	teaspoon dry thyme

Preheat oven to 350 degrees. Lightly spray a 10-by-6-inch baking dish with vegetable cooking spray.

Combine all ingredients and pour into the prepared dish. Bake uncovered 20–25 minutes, or until a knife inserted near the center comes out clean.

Pour the mixture into the dish and bake, uncovered, for about 20–25 minutes, or, until an inserted knife comes out clean. Serves 6.

Edamame Garlic Succotash

Edamame comes in pods, like peas. You can either buy it fresh and shell it, or look for frozen, already shelled.

2 tablespoons cornstarch
3 cups low-fat milk or plain soymilk
1 head of garlic, cloves peeled and chopped
½ cup shelled edamame beans
½ cup fresh or frozen corn
1 red bell pepper, diced
½ cup kidney beans
 Sea salt and black pepper to taste
½ cup sliced green onions

Mix the cornstarch into the milk or soymilk until dissolved and pour into a large saucepan. Add the garlic and bring just to a boil. Reduce heat to medium and simmer, whisking constantly, for 1 minute. Remove from heat, let cool, and strain, reserving the milk. In a blender, puree the garlic, adding small amounts of the reserved milk as needed until the garlic mixture is smooth and creamy.

Toss the edamame, corn, red pepper, and kidney beans into another saucepan and add just enough of the garlic cream to cover. Simmer, covered, over medium-low heat for 4–5 minutes, stirring frequently. Season with salt and pepper as desired. Top with the green onions and serve. Serves 4.

Note: Adding a little grated low-fat sharp cheddar would make this side dish orgasmic.

Roasted Pumpkin

*Pumpkins are not just for pies and jack-o-lanterns! Brimming
with iron, folate, calcium, and fiber, these golden globes are
great for heart attack prevention. This new trick with
pumpkin is a treat your family will want again.*

1   small pumpkin (2–pounds), peeled, seeded, and cut into 1-
      inch cubes
1   medium onion, chopped
½   teaspoon each of cinnamon and fresh-grated nutmeg
     Sea salt to taste
     Maple syrup

Preheat oven to 350 degrees. In a mixing bowl toss together the
pumpkin, onion, spices, and just enough maple syrup to coat evenly.
Place the mixture into a shallow roasting pan and roast for 20–30
minutes or until pumpkin is tender. Serves 4.

Note: For easy peeling, cut the pumpkin into wedges and use a
potato peeler to trim the skin off. And don't discard the seeds:
Sprinkle a little seasoning on them and roast them for a crunchy
snack.

Sweet Potato Casserole

I yam what I yam.

8   medium sweet potatoes
1   cup fresh pineapple chunks
1/2   cup toasted pecan pieces
1   teaspoon vanilla
1   cup Sucanat
1/2   cup pineapple juice

Preheat oven to 375 degrees. Oven-roast the sweet potatoes until half-baked.

Cut the potatoes, skin and all, into half-inch slices and arrange them in a baking dish. Layer alternately with pineapple, pecans, and Sucanat.

Pour the pineapple juice over all and bake 30 minutes, or until the sweet potatoes are done. If it turns you on, sprinkle some crunchy cereal such as Grape Nuts or granola over the top before you add the juice. Serves 8–10.

North African Sweet Potato Pancakes

Use these as an appetizer at your next wine party,
accompanied by a creative dipping sauce.

2½ pounds sweet potatoes, peeled and grated
1¼ cups liquid egg substitute, or 9 egg whites, lightly beaten
1 medium onion, finely minced
2 tablespoons wheat germ
2 tablespoons whole-wheat flour
1 tablespoon fresh rosemary, chopped (leaves only)
1½ teaspoon sea salt
½ teaspoon white pepper
Peanut oil for frying

In a large bowl, combine the grated sweet potatoes and egg whites or egg substitute. Add the onion, wheat germ, flour, rosemary, salt, and pepper and mix well. Cover and refrigerate 2–4 hours. Be patient.

In a large skillet, over medium heat, heat enough peanut oil to cover the bottom. Scoop the batter by about ¼-cup portions into the pan. Do not overcrowd.

Cook until crispy and brown on one side, then carefully turn and continue cooking until the other side is crispy and brown. Drain on paper toweling, and serve warm. Makes 26 pancakes.

Desserts

If there is to be peace in the world,
    There must be peace in the nations.
If there is to be peace in the nations,
    There must be peace in the cities.
If there is to be peace in the cities,
    There must be peace between neighbors.
If there is to be peace between neighbors,
    There must be peace in the home.
If there is to be peace in the home,
    There must be peace in the heart.

—Lao-tse, Chinese philosopher, sixth-century B.C.

Apples Foster

*You've had bananas Foster, the New Orleans tradition,
but I bet you've never considered using fall apples in
this classic romantic dish. Serve it over low-fat vanilla
ice cream or angel food cake.*

 $^1\!/_2$ cup butter or Smart Balance Buttery Spread
 1   cup Sucanat or brown sugar
 $^1\!/_2$ teaspoon cinnamon
 4   Granny Smith apples, cored and diced small (don't peel them!)
 $^1\!/_2$ cup apple jack or apple brandy
 $^1\!/_8$ cup rum

In a large skillet, combine the butter or Smart Balance, Sucanat or
sugar, and cinnamon. Heat over low heat, stirring constantly, until
the sugar dissolves. Add the apples and apple jack liquor, and
continue cooking until the apples are tender and beginning to brown.
Add the rum and very carefully ignite it. When the flames die down,
spoon generous portions of the molten concoction over low-fat
vanilla ice cream or angel food cake. Serves 4.

Poached Pears

2	pears, peeled and cored
1	cup dry red wine
1	cup water
1	teaspoon cinnamon
$^1/_8$	teaspoon nutmeg
3	tablespoons honey

Place the pears, wine, and water in a nonreactive saucepan, making sure the liquid covers the pears completely. Bring just to a boil, then reduce heat to medium-low and simmer, covered, about 15 minutes, or until the pears are fork tender. Remove pears from the liquid with a slotted spoon, and serve with Berry Ketchup (page 151).

Melon in Rum-Lime Sauce

*A crunchy biscotti is the perfect companion to
this summer delight.*

1 cantaloupe
1 small honeydew melon
⅓ watermelon
1 cup fresh blueberries
⅔ cup fructose sweetener
1 teaspoon grated lime zest
⅓ cup water
⅓ cup lime juice
½ cup light rum
1 tablespoon Midori melon liqueur

Cut the melons into bite-size pieces. Arrange the melon pieces and blueberries on a serving platter.

In a nonreactive saucepan, combine the water and fructose sweetener. Bring it just to a boil and add the rum, Midori liqueur, lime juice, and lime zest. If you wish a somewhat thicker sauce, make a slurry of 1 tablespoon cornstarch and 1 tablespoon water. Add the slurry a tiny bit at a time—you don't want the sauce too thick.

Allow the sauce to cool and pour it over the arranged fruit, then refrigerate for at least 1 hour. Garnish with mint sprigs or edible garden flowers.

Indian Pudding

- 1 tablespoon vegetable oil
- 1 cup raisins
  Brewed tea
- 5 cups plain soymilk, divided use
- 1/2 cup cornmeal
- 1 tablespoon brown rice syrup
- 1/4 cup maple syrup
- 1 teaspoon fresh ginger, minced
- 1/2 cup slivered almonds
  Sea salt to taste

Preheat the oven to 350 degrees. Coat a 1½-quart baking dish with the oil.

Place the raisins in a bowl with just enough tea to cover and let soak 15 minutes. Drain well and set aside.

In a heavy saucepan, combine 4 cups of soymilk and the cornmeal. Heat over medium heat, stirring constantly, for 5 minutes. Add the syrups, ginger, almonds, raisins, and salt.

Pour the mixture into the prepared baking dish, and add the remaining cup of soymilk. Stir a few strokes. Bake for 30 minutes, and turn off the oven. Leave the pudding in the oven, with the door closed, until the oven is cool. Your patience will be rewarded.

Serve this decadent pudding hot or cold. Serves 4.

Berry Good Tiramisu

1   cup each raspberries, blueberries, blackberries, and
        strawberries
1   cup Sucanat or $\frac{1}{8}$ cup stevia powder
    Juice of 1 lemon
2   cups vanilla soymilk
8   ounces nonfat sour cream
8   ounces Yogurt Cheese, made with vanilla yogurt (method
        follows)
1   10-inch angel food cake
1   cup berry liqueur of choice (such as Chambord)
    Fresh mint sprigs

In a mixing bowl combine the berries, sweetener, and lemon juice.
Mash the berries with a fork. Refrigerate for at least 1 hour.

In another bowl, combine the sour cream and yogurt cheese and
gently mix until blended.

To assemble, place a layer of cake in the bottom of a large glass or
crystal bowl and brush with the liqueur. Spread a third of the yogurt-
sour cream mixture, followed by a third of the berry mixture. Repeat
the layering 2 more times. Refrigerate for at least 1 hour. Serve
topped with a dollop of nonfat sour cream and a mint sprig.
Serves 12.

Yogurt Cheese

This is a sinfully delicious alternative to cream cheese and sour
cream. Be sure to use only yogurts (vanilla for desserts, or plain) that
don't have the gelatins often found in many of the flavored yogurts.

Spoon yogurt into a fine mesh strainer lined with either a double thickness of cheesecloth or an unbleached coffee filter. Place the strainer over a bowl to catch the liquid as it separates from the yogurt. Cover and place in the refrigerator for at least 8 hours. A pint of yogurt will yield about 1 cup of cheese.

Mix with fruit as desired, or with Parmesan cheese for a great garlic bread topper.

Skinny Pumpkin Pie

    4   egg whites, slightly beaten
    1   16-ounce can pumpkin
    1   tablespoon wheat germ
 $^1/_2$ cup Sucanat
    2   tablespoon maple syrup
    1   tablespoon cornstarch
 $^1/_2$ teaspoon sea salt
 $^1/_2$ teaspoon cinnamon
 $^1/_2$ teaspoon pumpkin pie spice
    1   12-ounce can evaporated skim milk
    1   Nut Crust Pastry shell (recipe follows)
         Soy Whipped Cream (recipe follows)

Preheat oven to 425 degrees. Whisk together the egg whites, pumpkin, wheat germ, sweeteners, cornstarch, salt, and spices. Be sure to whisk till the cornstarch dissolves. Pour into the pie shell and bake for 15 minutes. Reduce the temperature to 350 degrees and bake for an additional 45 minutes, or until a knife inserted near the center comes out clean. Makes a 9-inch pie.

Nut Crust Pastry

 $1^1/_2$ cups whole wheat flour
    1   teaspoon sea salt
 $^1/_2$ cup finely chopped nuts
 $^1/_2$ cup vegetable oil
    3   tablespoons plain soymilk

Combine the flour, salt, and nuts, and blend well. Combine the oil and soymilk and add to the flour mixture all at once. Blend until the

mixture holds together. Gently shape into a ball and flatten. Roll the crust out between 2 sheets of waxed paper to about 12 inches diameter.

Carefully peel off one sheet of waxed paper and invert the crust into a 9-inch pie plate. Peel off the second sheet of paper. Ease the crust into the dish, crimp the edges, and fill.

NOTE: If you intend to use the crust for a no-bake pie, prick the bottom with a fork and bake about 15 minutes. Let cool and fill.

Soy Whipped Cream

Whipped cream is another of those foods we can't seem to live without, even though we might live a bit longer without it. This is a tasty alternative.

$3/4$ cup soymilk (Edensoy Extra Original preferred)
2 tablespoons honey
$1/2$ teaspoon vanilla
    Pinch of sea salt (optional)
$3/4$ cup safflower oil
$1/8$ teaspoon lemon juice

Combine the first 4 ingredients in a blender and process on high for 5–10 seconds. Slowly dribble in the oil, blending for a full minute after all the oil has been added. Fold in the lemon juice. Put into a covered container and chill. Makes 2 cups.

Terry's Tomato Soup Spice Cake

If you like spice cakes, you'll dig this version. Always remember to add dry ingredients to wet when making cakes, breads, or any other baked goods.

2   cups unbleached all-purpose flour
2   teaspoons non-aluminum baking powder
1   teaspoon cinnamon
1   teaspoon nutmeg
1/2   teaspoon ground cloves
1/2   cup liquid egg substitute
3/4   cup Sucanat
1   teaspoon vanilla
1   10-ounce can cream of tomato soup
1/2   cup chopped walnuts

Preheat oven to 350 degrees. Spray a 5-by-8-inch loaf pan with vegetable cooking spray, and lightly dust with flour.

Sift together the flour, baking powder, cinnamon, nutmeg, and cloves into a mixing bowl. Combine the egg substitute, Sucanat, vanilla, and tomato soup. Gradually add the flour mixture to the liquid mix and mix until well blended. Fold in the walnuts.

Pour into the prepared pan and bake for 25–30 minutes, or until a toothpick comes out clean.

Blueberry Muffins

1	cup buckwheat flour, sifted
1	cup brown rice flour, sifted
1/4	cup wheat germ
1	tablespoon aluminum-free baking powder
1/2	teaspoon sea salt
2	large ripe bananas
1/3	cup vegetable oil
1/4	cup maple syrup
1/2	cup soymilk
1	cup blueberries
1/4	cup chopped walnuts
	Zest of one lemon

Preheat oven to 350 degrees. Spray muffin tins with vegetable cooking spray.

Combine the flours, wheat germ, baking powder, and salt in a large mixing bowl.

In another bowl, mash the dickens out of the bananas. Add the oil, maple syrup, and soymilk, and mix just until blended. Add the banana mixture to the dry ingredients and blend gently. Fold in the blueberries and lemon zest.

Spoon the mixture into the prepared muffin tins, filling to about three-quarters. Bake for 35 minutes or until a toothpick comes out clean. Makes 12 muffins.

Carrot Muffins

¹/₂ cup raisins
     Brewed tea
  1 cup buckwheat flour, sifted
  1 cup brown rice flour, sifted
¹/₄ cup wheat germ
  2 teaspoons aluminum-free baking soda
  1 teaspoon cinnamon
¹/₂ teaspoon sea salt
  1 teaspoon stevia powder
³/₄ cup vanilla soy or rice milk
¹/₃ cup vegetable oil
¹/₄ cup maple syrup
  1 cup grated carrot
¹/₂ cup chopped walnuts

Preheat oven to 350 degrees. Spray a muffin tin with vegetable cooking spray.

Combine the raisins with just enough tea to cover and let soak for 15 minutes. Drain well and set aside. In a large mixing bowl, mix the flours, wheat germ, baking powder, cinnamon, and salt.

In another mixing bowl, combine the stevia with the milk and stir until it dissolves. Add the oil and syrup and mix well. Add the mixture to the dry ingredients and mix just until blended. Fold in the carrots, raisins, and walnuts. (Be careful not to over-mix or the muffins will come out like hockey pucks!)

Spoon the mixture into the prepared muffin tin, filling about three-fourths. Bake 35 minutes or until a toothpick comes out clean. Makes 12 muffins.

"90–10" Chocolate Chip Cookies

*It's impossible to recreate a classic chocolate chip cookie
without using some form of sugar. But occasional "cheating"
is perfectly acceptable as long as you practice moderation and
maintain a healthy relationship with treats and keep them in
perspective. So, if we're good 90 percent of the time, the 10
percent of time when we cheat will take care of itself.*

1³/4 cups all-purpose flour
²/3 cup powdered sugar (organic preferred)
¹/3 cup good-quality cocoa powder
2¹/4 teaspoons aluminum-free baking powder
¹/4 teaspoon sea salt
3 tablespoons melted butter or Smart Balance Buttery Spread
¹/2 cup Sucanat
1 tablespoon vanilla
2¹/2 tablespoons maple syrup
3 egg whites, lightly beaten
¹/4 cup semisweet chocolate chips or carob chips
¹/2 cup nuts (walnuts or pecans, your choice)

Sift the dry ingredients together in a large mixing bowl. In another
bowl, combine the butter or Smart Balance, Sucanat, vanilla, syrup,
and egg whites, and add to the dry ingredients, blending well. Fold in
the chocolate chips and nuts. Cover and refrigerate for 30 minutes.

Preheat oven to 350 degrees. Drop the cookie mixture by spoonfuls
onto a baking sheet lightly sprayed with vegetable cooking spray.
Bake for 8 minutes. Cool and consume. Makes about 2 dozen cookies.

Chocolate Sauce

*We must be diligent and never forget that
chocolate is a vegetable!*

¹/₂   cup good quality cocoa powder
¹/₂   cup Sucanat
¹/₄   cup strong brewed coffee
¹/₂   cup low-fat milk or plain soy milk
 1   teaspoon vanilla
¹/₄   teaspoon sea salt
 1   tablespoon unbleached all-purpose flour

Combine the cocoa, Sucanat, coffee, milk, vanilla, and salt in a saucepan. Heat over medium heat, whisking constantly until the sauce becomes smooth as silk. Add the flour and whisk for another minute. Just as the sauce begins to thicken, remove it from the heat. Makes 1 cup.

Tiffany's Cream Cheese Spread

 1   8-ounce package low-fat cream cheese, softened
 2   tablespoons honey
 2   teaspoons vanilla

Combine all ingredients and beat the dickens out of them with an electric mixer until the mixture becomes creamy and spreadable. Makes 1 cup.

NOTE: For extra oomph, add a few tablespoons of cocoa powder, but first warm it up in the honey and whisk to dissolve it, then add to the spread. A handful of chopped, toasted walnuts really jazzes it up!

ABOUT THE AUTHOR

Chef Wendell Fowler, author of *Eat Right, Now!* (Guild Press-Emmis Publishing, 2002) and nationally syndicated health columnist, is an expert in the field of the culinary healing arts and believes that chefs can be the doctors of the future.

In 1988, Fowler was diagnosed with viral cardiomyopathy. That brush with death led to a major lifestyle change resulting in the loss of a whopping one hundred pounds of excess weight. This motivated him to dedicate his life to sharing his miracle and his epiphany that our "Earth Suits" are the most precious possessions we have, and that we need to be good stewards of them.

A compelling and humorous motivational speaker and media personality, Fowler has energetically carried his "food as medicine" message via many Indianapolis-area radio and television stations, and more recently on the World Wide Web at EatRightNow.net.

His popular syndicated column, which has appeared in *Indianapolis Prime Times* for two years, won the 2001 Gold Medal for Seniors Issues from the North America Mature Publishers Association (NAMPA). The judges' comments: "Fowler's 'Preventive Measures' column does the seemingly impossible—it presents truly helpful information with panache. A bit of history, a bit of attitude and lots of nutritional advice are served up in a loving format." In 2002 and 2003, Fowler won several more NAMPA awards.

Fowler has been the proprietor of Fowler's Catering for more than two decades, serving both social and corporate affairs. He also has operated Fowler's Airport Catering since 1992 and is the official caterer for the National Basketball Association in Indianapolis.

He takes his craft quite seriously, and has competed and medaled in several sanctioned American Culinary Federation competitions and has received many kudos for his high quality, upscale, farm-fresh, organic foods. Fowler defends, promotes and supports the organic farm community in Indiana and believes that family farmer is the backbone of America.

AWARDS AND ACCOMPLISHMENTS

- GOLD MEDAL—North America Mature Publishers Association. 2001 GOLD AWARD—Preventive Measures, *Indianapolis Prime Times*.

- SILVER MEDAL—North America Mature Publishers Association. 2001 SILVER AWARD—Preventive Measures, *Indianapolis Prime Times*.

- SECOND PLACE—North America Mature Publishers Association. 2002 SECOND PLACE AWARD—Preventive Measures, *Indianapolis Prime Times*.

- MERIT AWARD—Magazine/Newspaper Article Series.

- 2002 NATIONAL MEDIA AWARDS in competition with nationally recognized publications such as *Modern Maturity*, *My Generation*, *New Choices*, and *Prevention* magazines.

- THE AMERICAN CULINARY ASSOCIATION INVITATIONAL COMPETITION—Bronze medal in the 1992 and 1993 competitions in Indianapolis, Indiana.

ॐ

CHEF WENDELL R. FOWLER
820 S. Noble Street
Indianapolis, Indiana 46203
317-635-7006

The Dawning of the Age of Asparagus
216

Index

A

APPLES
Apples Foster, 202
Toasted Apple and Bleu Cheese
Wrap with Walnuts and Wild
Greens, 116
Warm Apple Cider Dressing, 147
ASIAN-STYLE DISHES
Asian "Beef" Noodle Salad, 167
Beans and Rice Asian-Style, 154
Gingered Barley, 166
Shiitake Noodles, 169
Singapore Noodles, 168
Yakisoba, 170
ASPARAGUS
Salsaparagus, 117

B

BARLEY
Gingered Barley, 166
Savory Sauerkraut and Barley
Casserole, 174
BASIC VEGETABLE STOCK, 128
BEANS AND LEGUMES
Beans and Rice Asian-Style, 154
El Pollo Loco Beans, 156
Mediterranean Garbanzo Beans, 158
"New" Old-Fashioned
Bean Salad, 136
Pinto Bean and Toasted
Corn Salsa, 122
Southern Black-Eyed Peas, 155
Tuscan Bean Soup, 132
Vegan Herbed White Bean
Spread, 118
Vegan Kidney Bean and Cashew
Bonanza, 159
BEANS, GREEN
Greek Green Beans, 193

Warm Green Bean and Mushroom
Salad, 137
BERRIES
Berry Good Tiramisu, 206
Berry Ketchup, 151
BEVERAGES
Mango Iced Tea, 126
Mayan Chocolate, 125
BROCCOLI
Broccoli Casserole, New Millennium
Style, 180
Broiled Cauliflower and
Broccoli, 192
BROWN RICE. See Rice.

C

CABBAGE
Creole Cabbage, 190
Crunchy Cabbage and Onion
Slaw, 142
Dutch Cole Slaw, 143
Hungarian Cabbage and
Potatoes, 189
Mashed Potatoes and Cabbage, 187
Sweet and Sour Red Cabbage, 191
CAKES
Terry's Tomato Soup Spice Cake, 210
CASHEWS
Vegan Kidney Bean and Cashew
Bonanza, 159
CASSEROLES
Broccoli Casserole, New Millennium
Style, 180
New Old-Fashioned Goulash
Casserole, 173
Savory Sauerkraut and Barley
Casserole, 174
Shepherd's Pie, 172
Spaghetti Florentine Casserole, 181

Give Peas a Chance!

Spinach-Rice Casserole with
Veggies, 182
CAULIFLOWER
Broiled Cauliflower and
Broccoli, 192
CHEESE
Toasted Apple and Bleu Cheese
Wrap with Walnuts and Wild
Greens, 116
Yogurt Cheese, 206
CHILE PEPPERS, HANDLING, 156–157
CHOCOLATE
"90–10" Chocolate Chip
Cookies, 213
Chocolate Lover's Logic, 40
Chocolate Sauce, 214
Mayan Chocolate, 125
COOKIES
"90–10" Chocolate Chip
Cookies, 213
CORN
Corn Chowder, 129
Pinto Bean and Toasted Corn
Salsa, 122
Quinoa Corn Chowder, 130
CRAB CAKES, MOCK, 121
CREAM CHEESE
Tiffany's Cream Cheese Spread, 214

D

DIPS AND SPREADS
Tiffany's Cream Cheese Spread, 214
Vegan Herbed White Bean
Spread, 118
DRESSINGS AND SAUCES
Berry Ketchup, 151
Chocolate Sauce, 214
Creamy Miso Dressing, 148
Flax Seed Vinaigrette, 147
Guacamole Salad Dressing, 149
Lime Marinade, 149
Melon in Rum-Lime Sauce, 204
Mushroom Gravy, 176

Mustard Dressing, 152
Sweet and Sour Dressing, 150
Vegetarian Mayonnaise, 152
Warm Apple Cider Dressing, 147

E

EDAMAME
Edamame Garlic Succotash, 197
"New" Old-Fashioned Bean Salad,
136
EGG SUBSTITUTES, 112–113
EGGPLANT
Indian Eggplant and Green
Peas, 194

F

"FAKE MEAT". See Seitan and wheat
meat.
FLAX SEED
Flax Seed Vinaigrette, 147
FLOUR SUBSTITUTE, 114

G

GOAT CHEESE
Summer Peach Salad with Goat
Cheese and Toasted Pecans, 146
GRANOLA
Basic Granola, 123
Granola Bars, 124
GRAVY
Mushroom Gravy, 176
GUACAMOLE
Guacamole Salad Dressing, 149

L

LATIN-STYLE DISHES
Cheese and Green Chile
Enchiladas, 179
El Pollo Loco Beans, 156
Mexican "Meatball" Soup, 133
Sizzling Tex-Mex Tempeh Stew, 134
Spicy Mexican Rice, 165
LIME
Lime Marinade, 149

M

MARINADES
Lime Marinade, 149
MAYONNAISE
Vegetarian Mayonnaise, 152
MELONS
Melon in Rum-Lime Sauce, 204
MILLET
Eureka Gold Potatoes, 186
MISO
Creamy Miso Dressing, 148
MOCK CRAB CAKES, 121
MUFFINS
Blueberry Muffins, 211
Carrot Muffins, 212
MUSHROOMS
Mushroom Gravy, 176
New Old-Fashioned Goulash
Casserole, 173
Shepherd's Pie, 172
Shiitake Noodles, 169
Vegetarian Stroganoff, 178
Vegetarian Swiss Steak, 175
Warm Green Bean and Mushroom
Salad, 137
MUSTARD
Mustard Dressing, 152

O

ONIONS
Crunchy Cabbage and Onion
Slaw, 142

P

PASTA
Asian "Beef" Noodle Salad, 167
Shiitake Noodles, 169
Singapore Noodles, 168
Spaghetti Florentine Casserole, 181
Yakisoba, 170
PEACHES
Summer Peach Salad with Goat
Cheese and Toasted Pecans, 146

PEARS
Poached Pears, 203
PEAS
Indian Eggplant and Green
Peas, 194
PECANS
Summer Peach Salad with Goat
Cheese and Toasted Pecans, 146
PIES
Nut Crust Pastry, 208
Shepherd's Pie, 172
Skinny Pumpkin Pie, 208
PIZZA DOUGH
Whole Wheat Pizza Dough, 184
POTATOES
Au Gratin Potatoes, 188
Baked American-Fried Potatoes, 119
Eureka Gold Potatoes, 186
Hungarian Cabbage and
Potatoes, 189
Indian Potato Patties, 120
Mashed Potatoes and Cabbage, 187
Oven-Roasted Potato Salad, 140
Summer Potato and Radish
Salad, 141
PUDDINGS
Indian Pudding, 205
PUMPKIN
nutritional facts, 110
Roasted Pumpkin, 198
Skinny Pumpkin Pie, 208

Q

QUINOA
Basic Quinoa, 160
Quinoa Corn Chowder, 130
Quinoa Pilaf, 161
Quinoa Vegetable Soup, 131

R

RADISHES
Summer Potato and Radish
Salad, 141

RICE
American Fried Rice, 164
Basic Brown Rice Pilaf, 163
Beans and Rice Asian-Style, 154
Brown Rice Salad with "Meat", 138
Pressure-Cooked Brown Rice, 162
Spicy Mexican Rice, 165
Spinach Bake Casserole, 196
Spinach-Rice Casserole with
    Veggies, 182

S

SALADS
Asian "Beef" Noodle Salad, 167
Brown Rice Salad with "Meat", 138
Crunchy Cabbage and Onion
    Slaw, 142
Dorothy's Sauerkraut Salad, 144
Dutch Cole Slaw, 143
"New" Old-Fashioned Bean Salad,
    136
Oven-Roasted Potato Salad, 140
"Sneaky" Chicken Salad, 145
Summer Peach Salad with Goat
    Cheese and Toasted Pecans, 146
Summer Potato and Radish
    Salad, 141
Warm Green Bean and Mushroom
    Salad, 137
SAUERKRAUT
Dorothy's Sauerkraut Salad, 144
Savory Sauerkraut and Barley
    Casserole, 174
SEITAN AND WHEAT MEAT
Asian "Beef" Noodle Salad, 167
Brown Rice Salad with "Meat", 138
"Meaty" Veggie Pot Roast, 176
Mexican "Meatball" Soup, 133
Vegetarian Stroganoff, 178
Vegetarian Swiss Steak, 175
Yakisoba, 170
SOUPS AND STEWS
Basic Vegetable Stock, 128
Corn Chowder, 129

Mexican "Meatball" Soup, 133
Quinoa Corn Chowder, 130
Quinoa Vegetable Soup, 131
Sizzling Tex-Mex Tempeh Stew, 134
Tuscan Bean Soup, 132
SOY WHIPPED CREAM, 209
SPINACH
Curried Spinach, 195
Spaghetti Florentine Casserole, 181
Spinach Bake Casserole, 196
Spinach-Rice Casserole with
    Veggies, 182
STEVIA, 114
STROGANOFF
Vegetarian Stroganoff, 178
SUCCOTASH
Edamame Garlic Succotash, 197
SWEET POTATOES
North African Sweet Potato
    Pancakes, 200
Sweet Potato Casserole, 199

T

TEA
Mango Iced Tea, 126
TEMPEH
Jerked Tempeh, 183
Sizzling Tex-Mex Tempeh Stew, 134
"Sneaky" Chicken Salad, 145
TIRAMISU
Berry Good Tiramisu, 206
TOFU
Cheese and Green Chile
    Enchiladas, 179

W

WALNUTS
Toasted Apple and Bleu Cheese
    Wrap with Walnuts and Wild
    Greens, 116

X

XYLITOL, 111–112

The Dawning of the Age of Asparagus